For my family
my infinite source of whimsical imagination

WHIMSICAL CHILDREN'S FANTASIES : A Juvenile Adult Coloring Book
Copyright © 2016 by Louis D. Wiyono & Davlin Publishing
Printed By CreateSpace, An Amazon.com Company
Available from Amazon.com, CreateSpace.com, and other retail outlets

ISBN-13: 978-1532720390
ISBN-10: 1532720394

www.davlinpublishing.com | www.artoflou.com

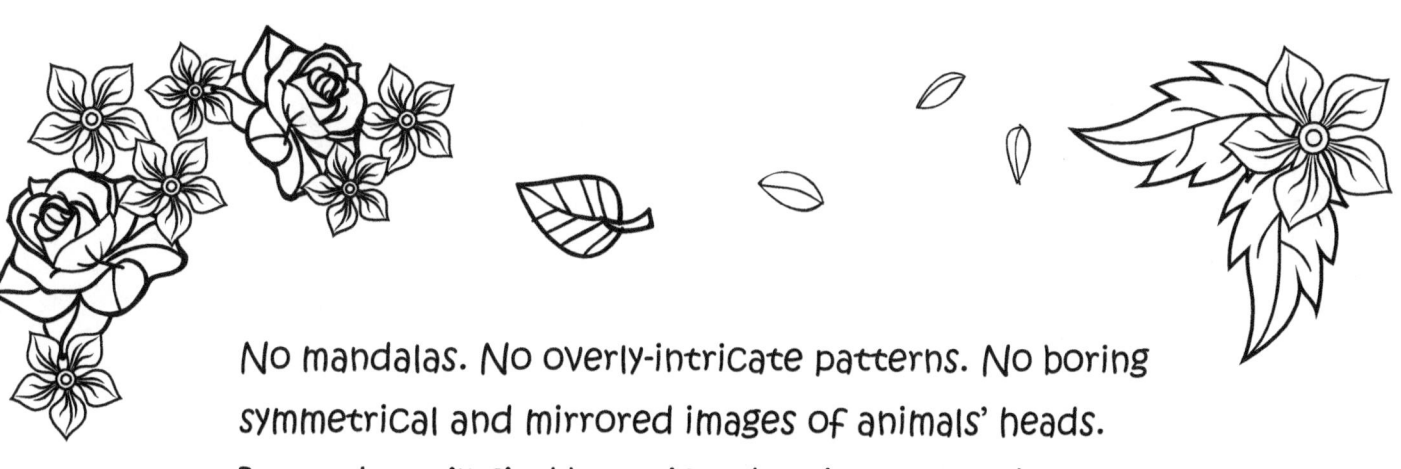

No mandalas. No overly-intricate patterns. No boring symmetrical and mirrored images of animals' heads. Instead, you'll find beautiful drawings of magical scenes filled with lovable characters and curious creatures.

From the tallest castle to the deep sea, from hot desert canyons to cool tropical bayou, from tranquil lake to sparkling city, there are a lot of magical places to see! Also, discover the most lovable characters and creatures along the way – a fishing bear, a flying whale and turtle, a boy and his pet dragon, a gypsy princess with her dancing dog – just to name a few.

Inspired by children's fantasies and drawn in classic children's book illustration style, this coloring book gives you a bundle of super fun pages dedicated to your coloring enjoyment!

Well, what are you waiting for? Grab your tools and start coloring your way through the whimsical world of children's fantasies!

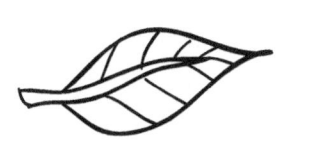
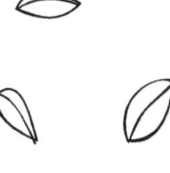
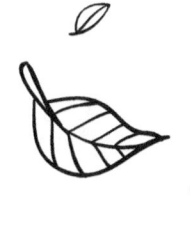

COLOR TEST PAGE

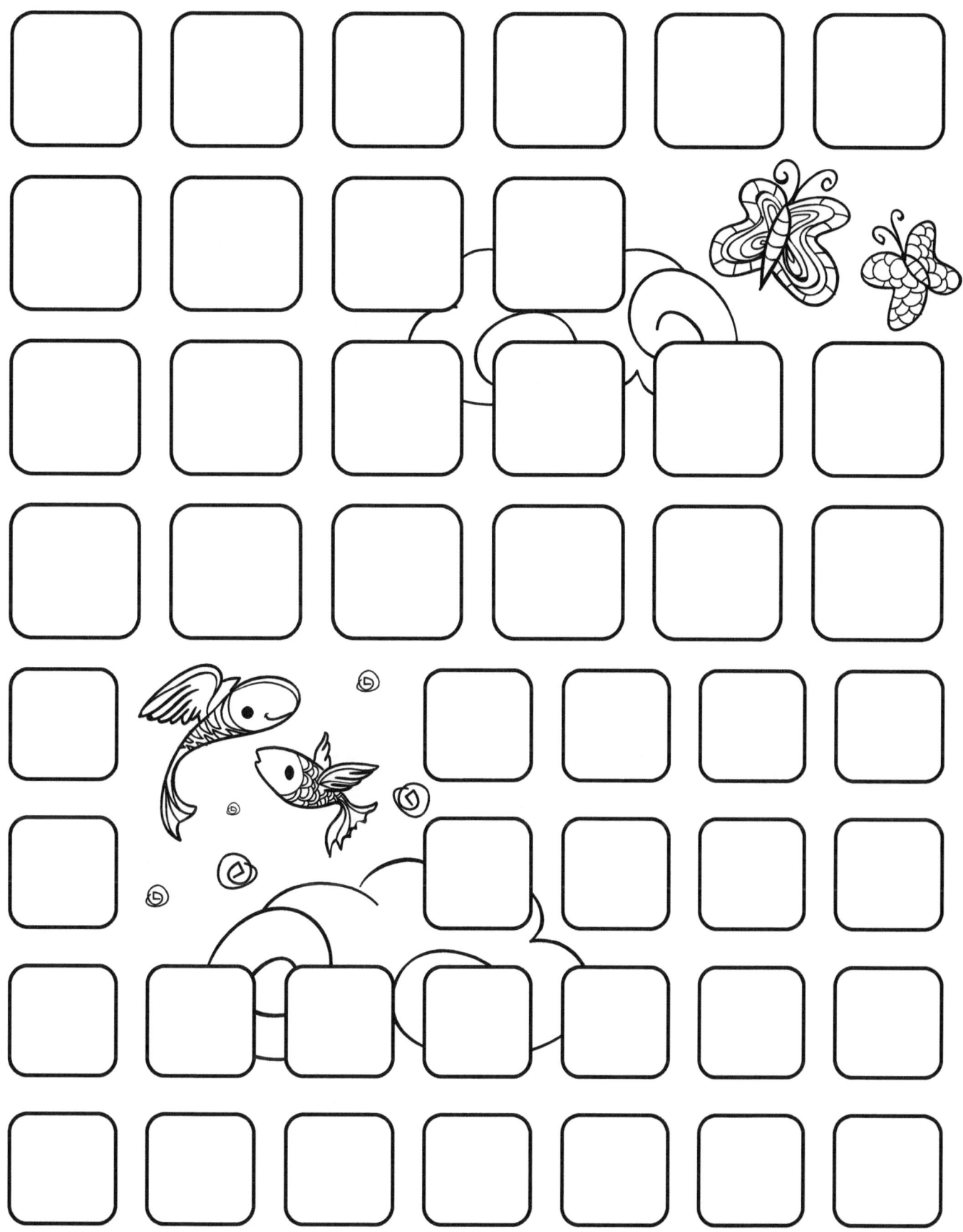

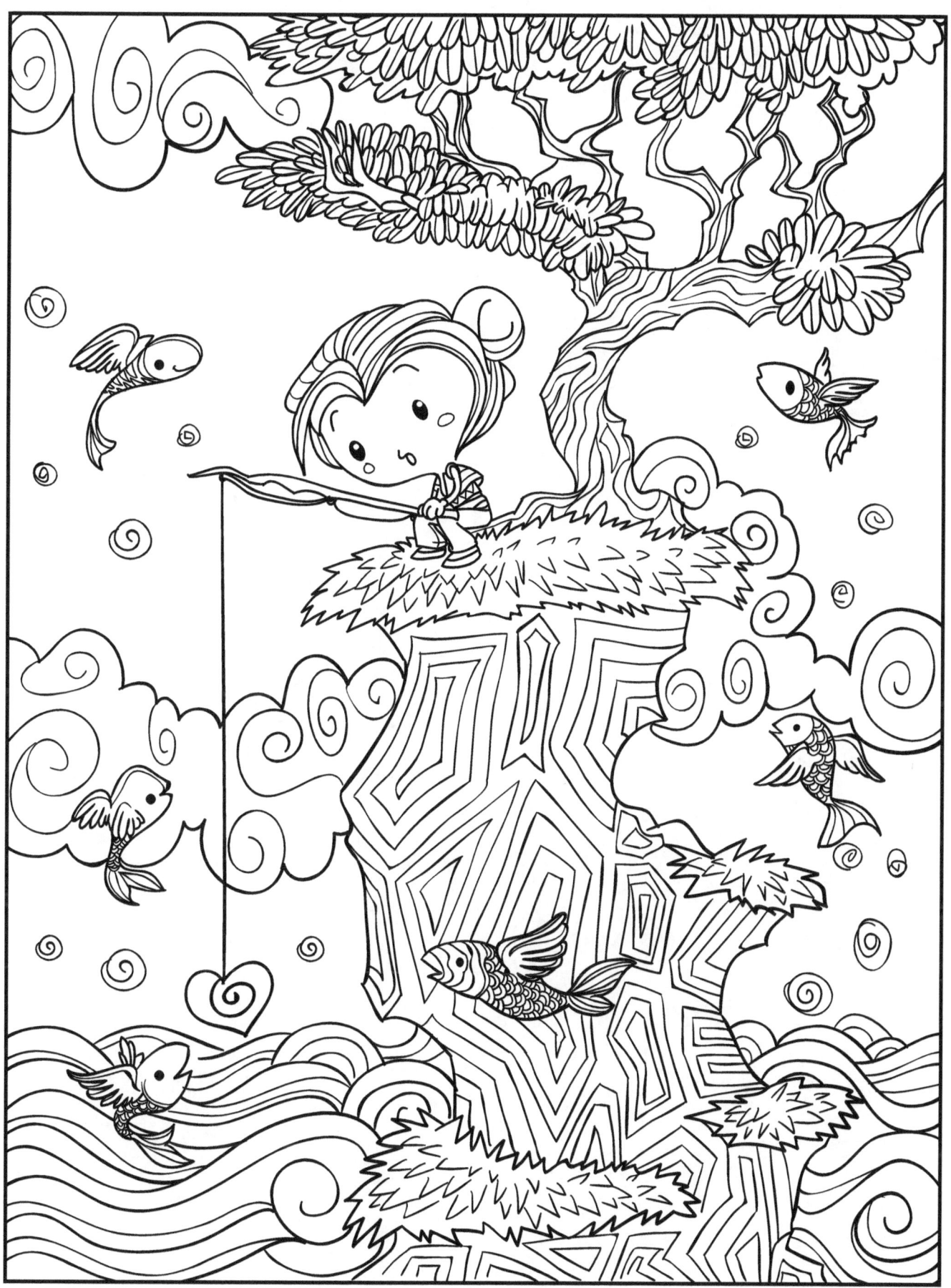

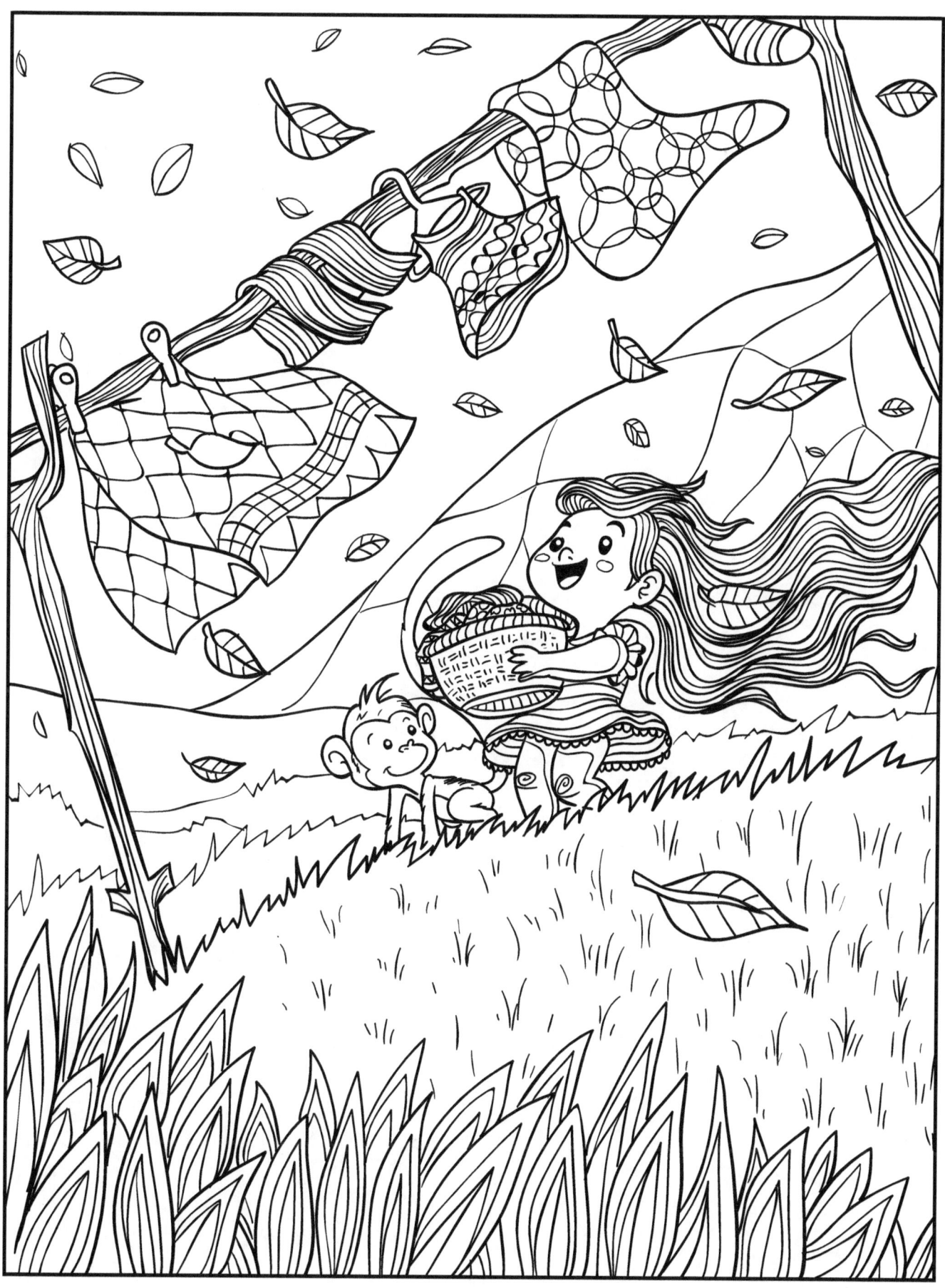

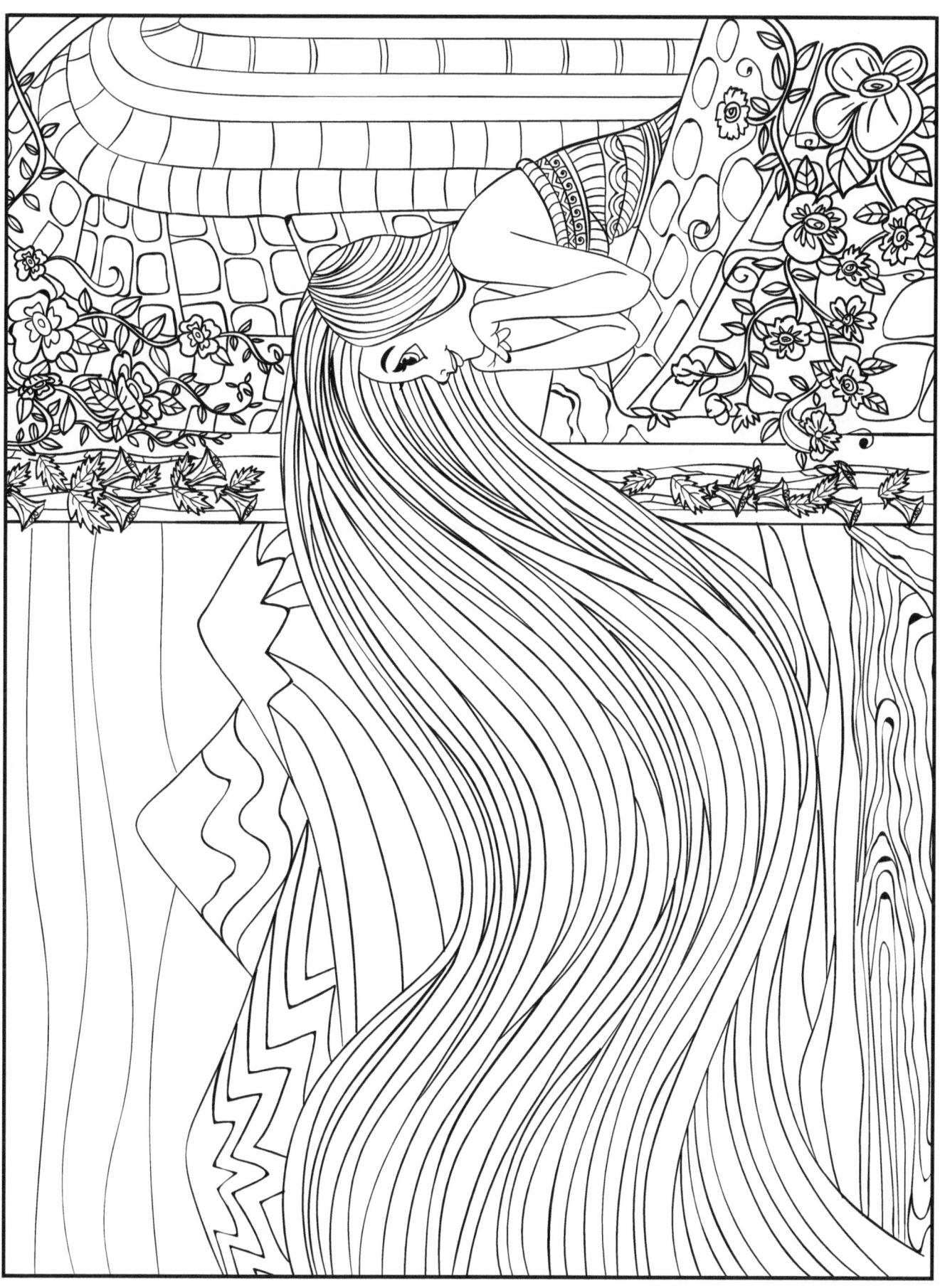

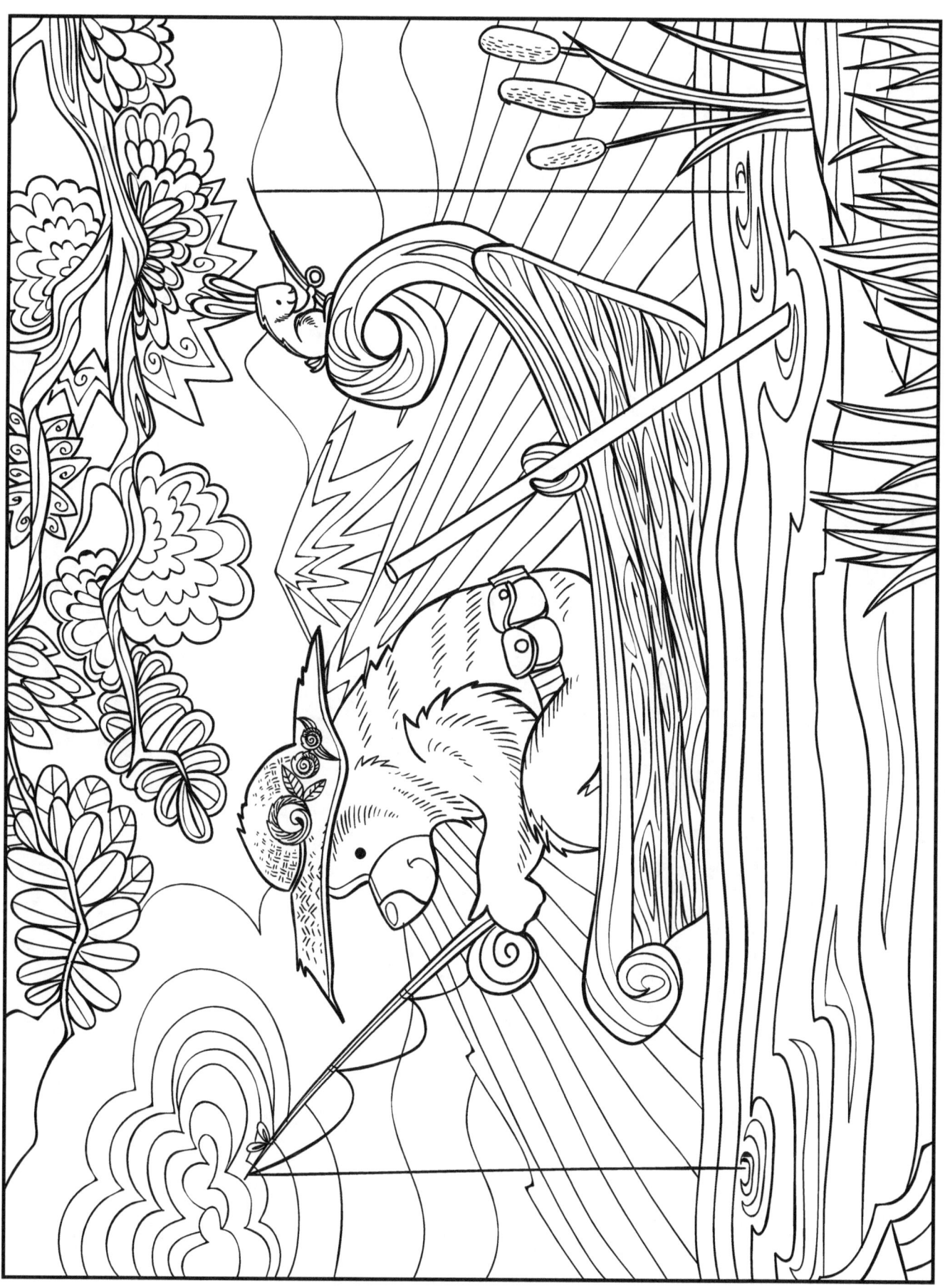

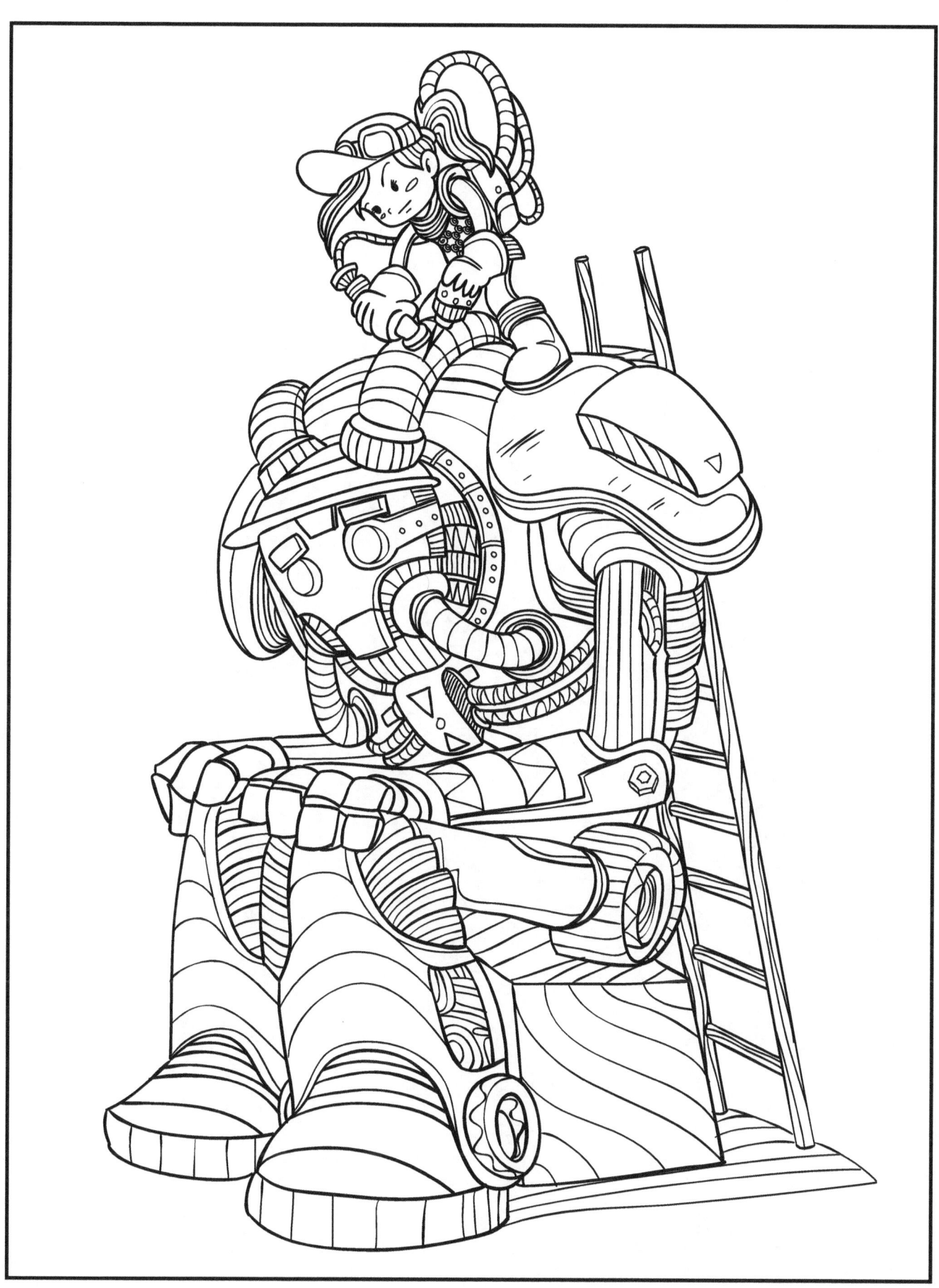

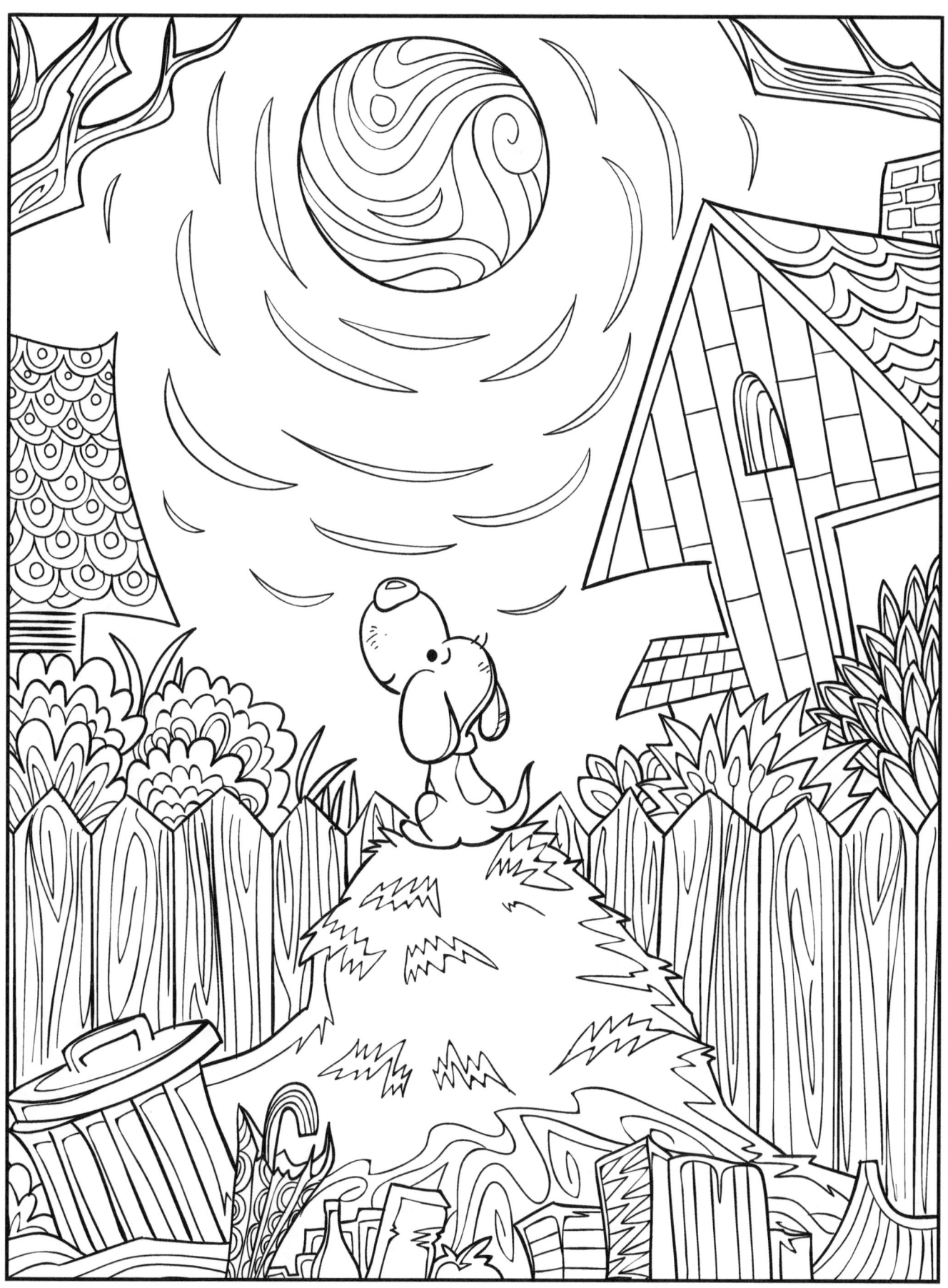

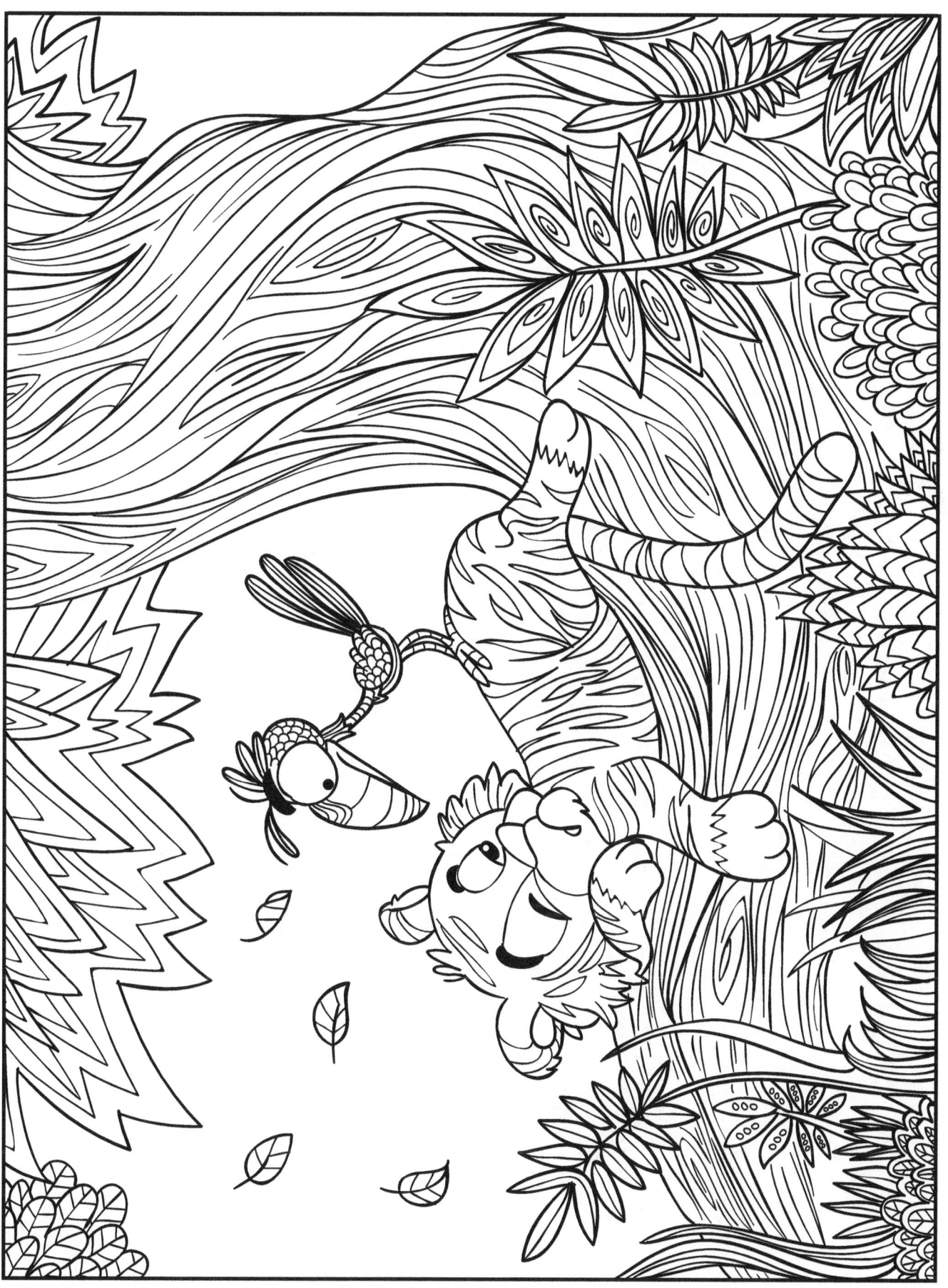

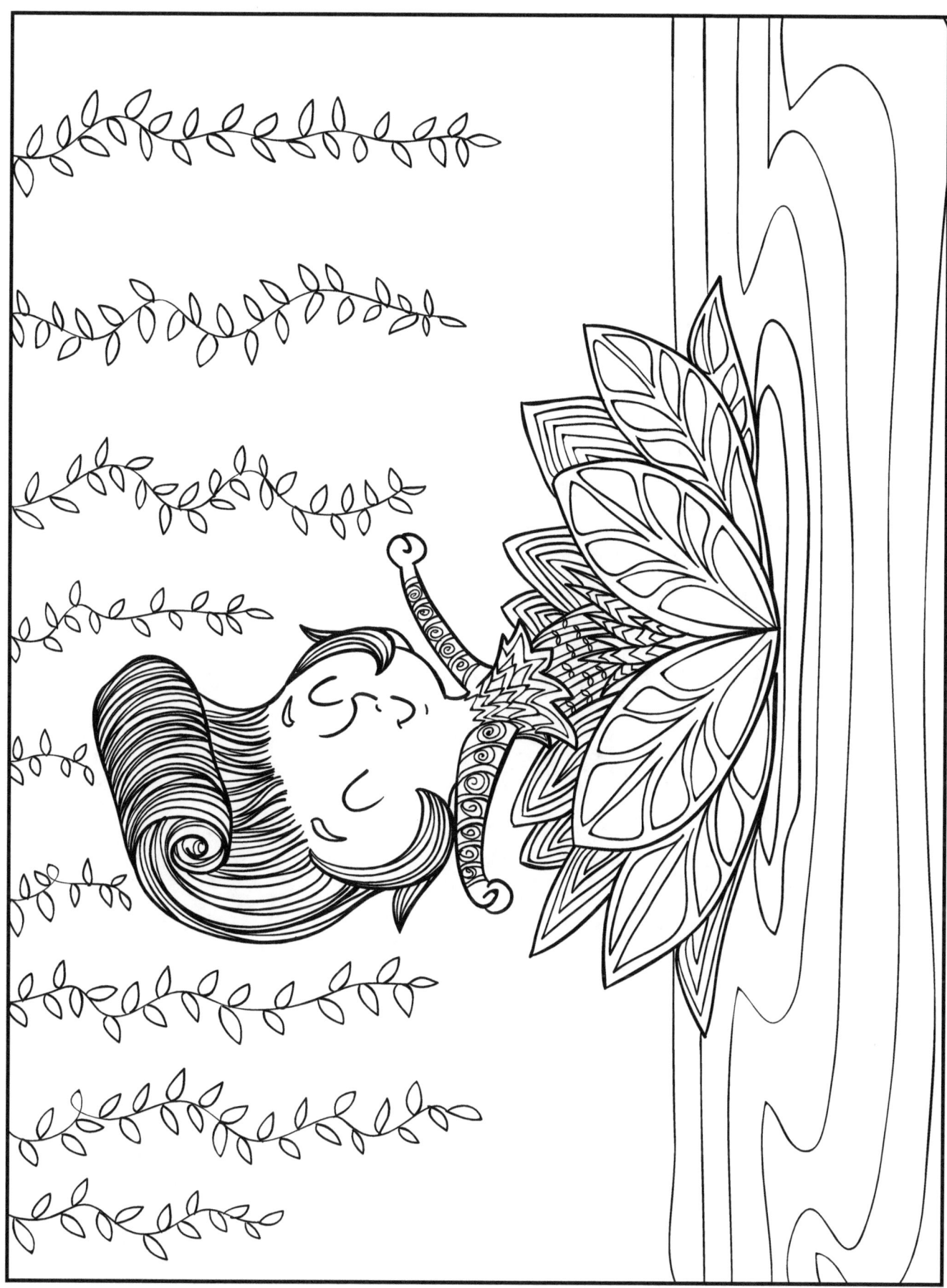

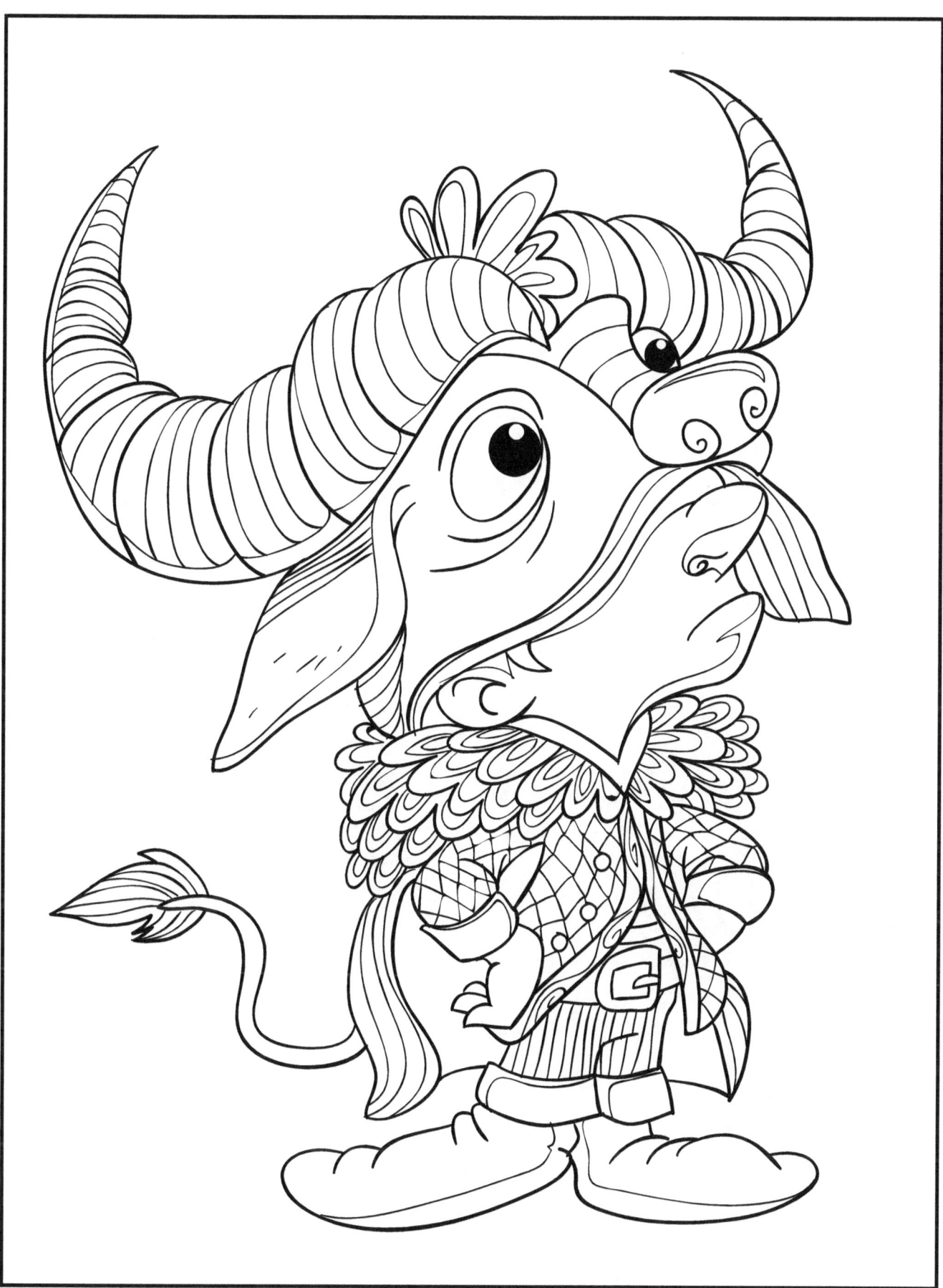

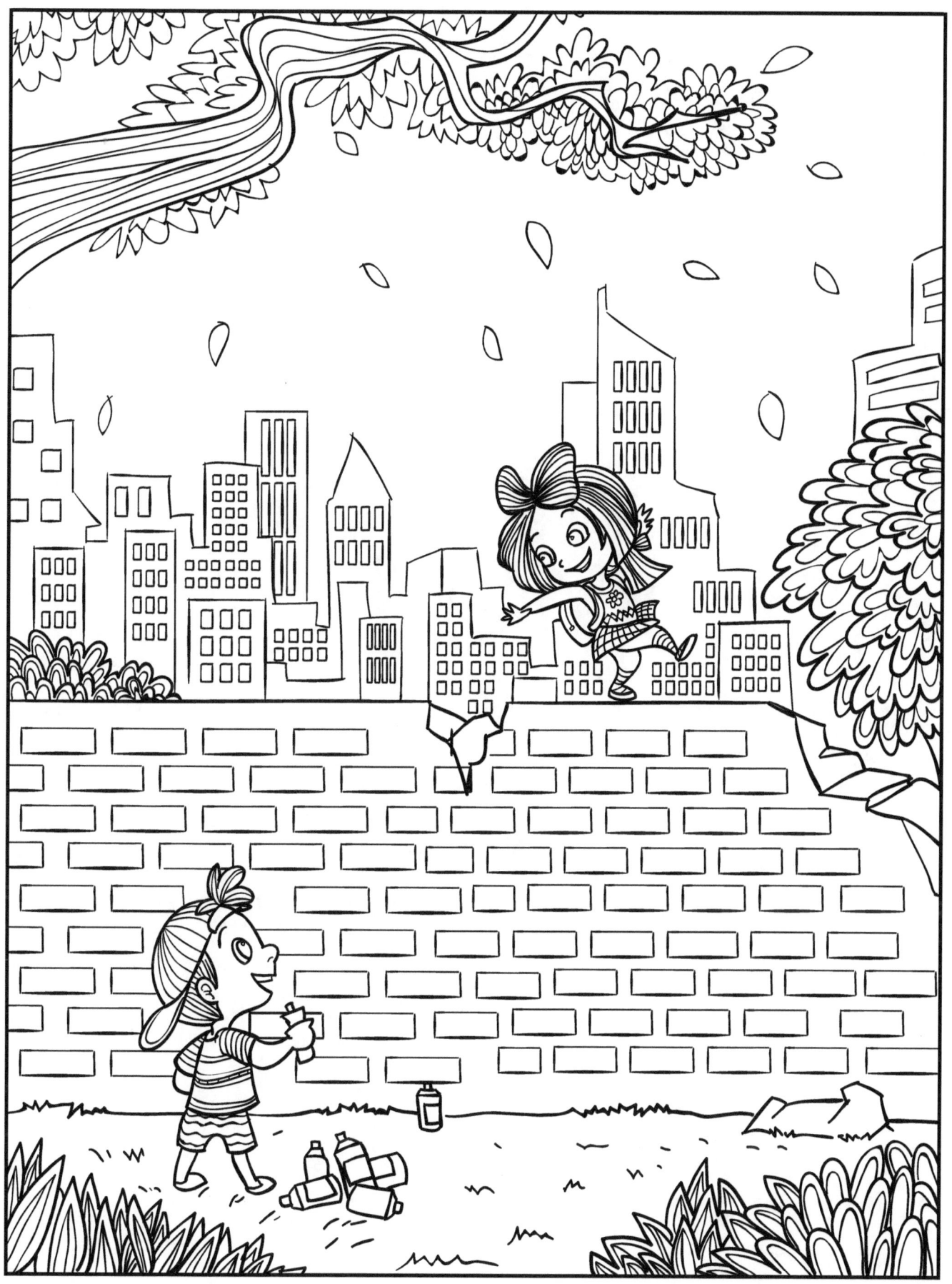

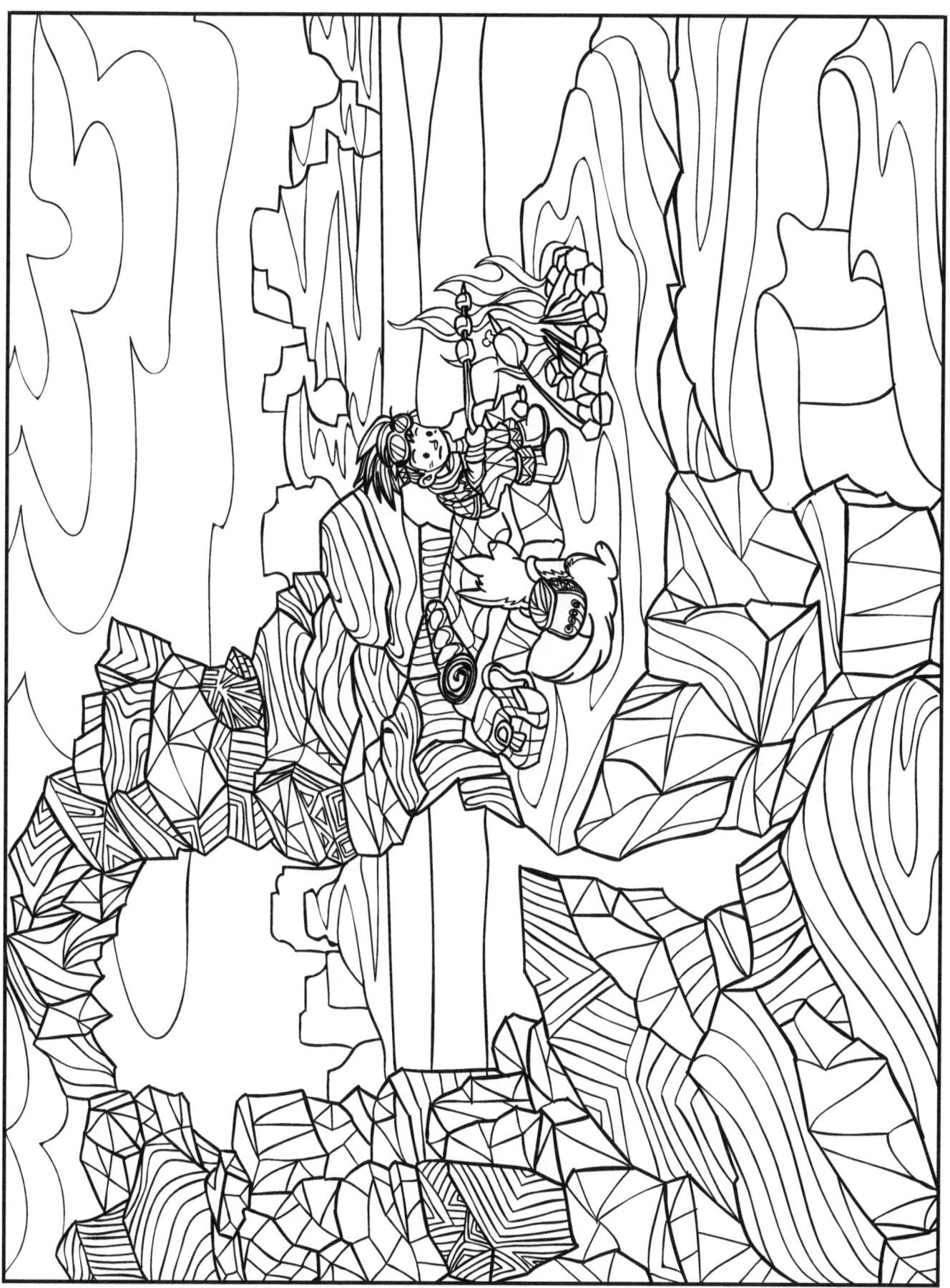

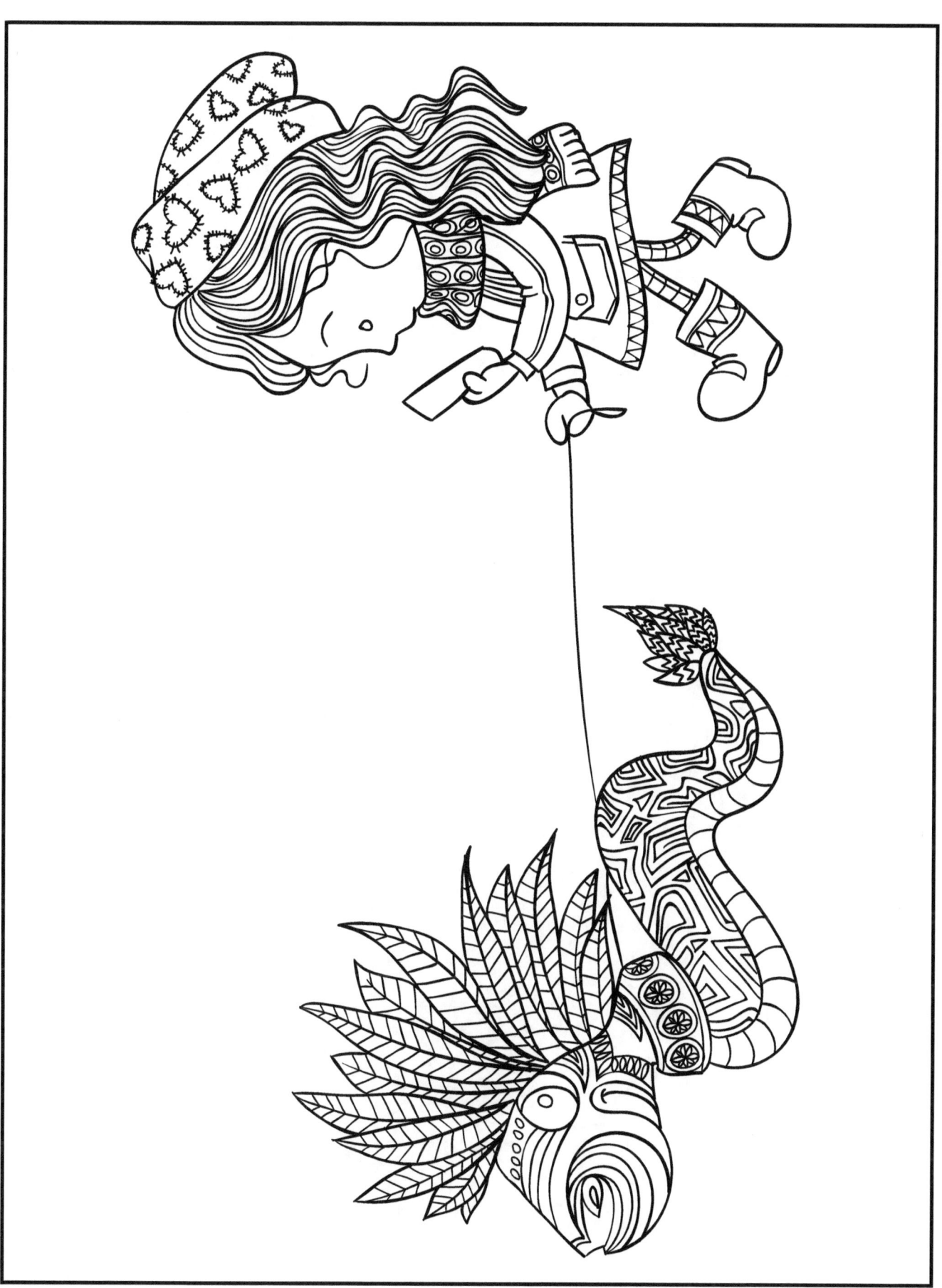

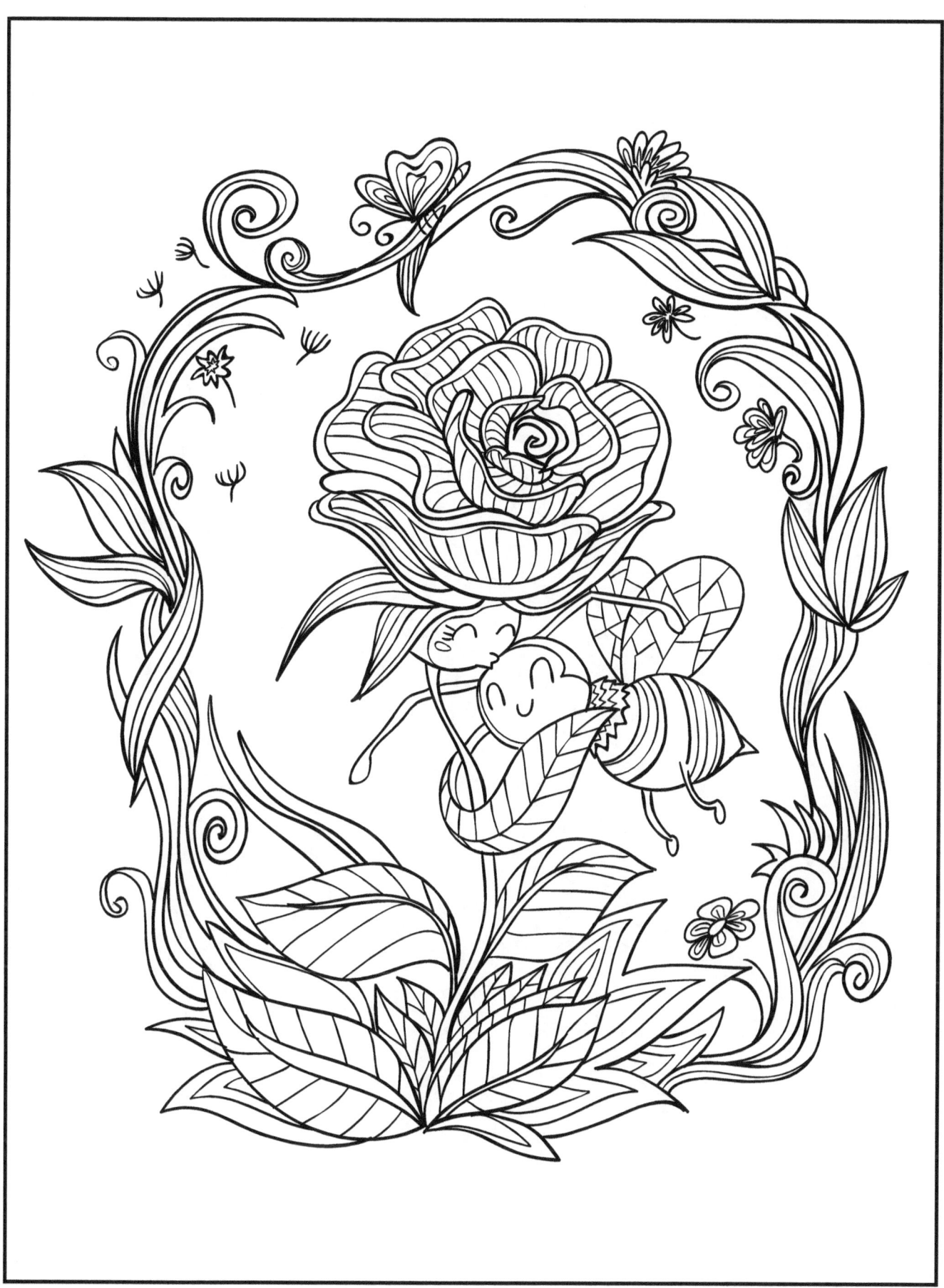

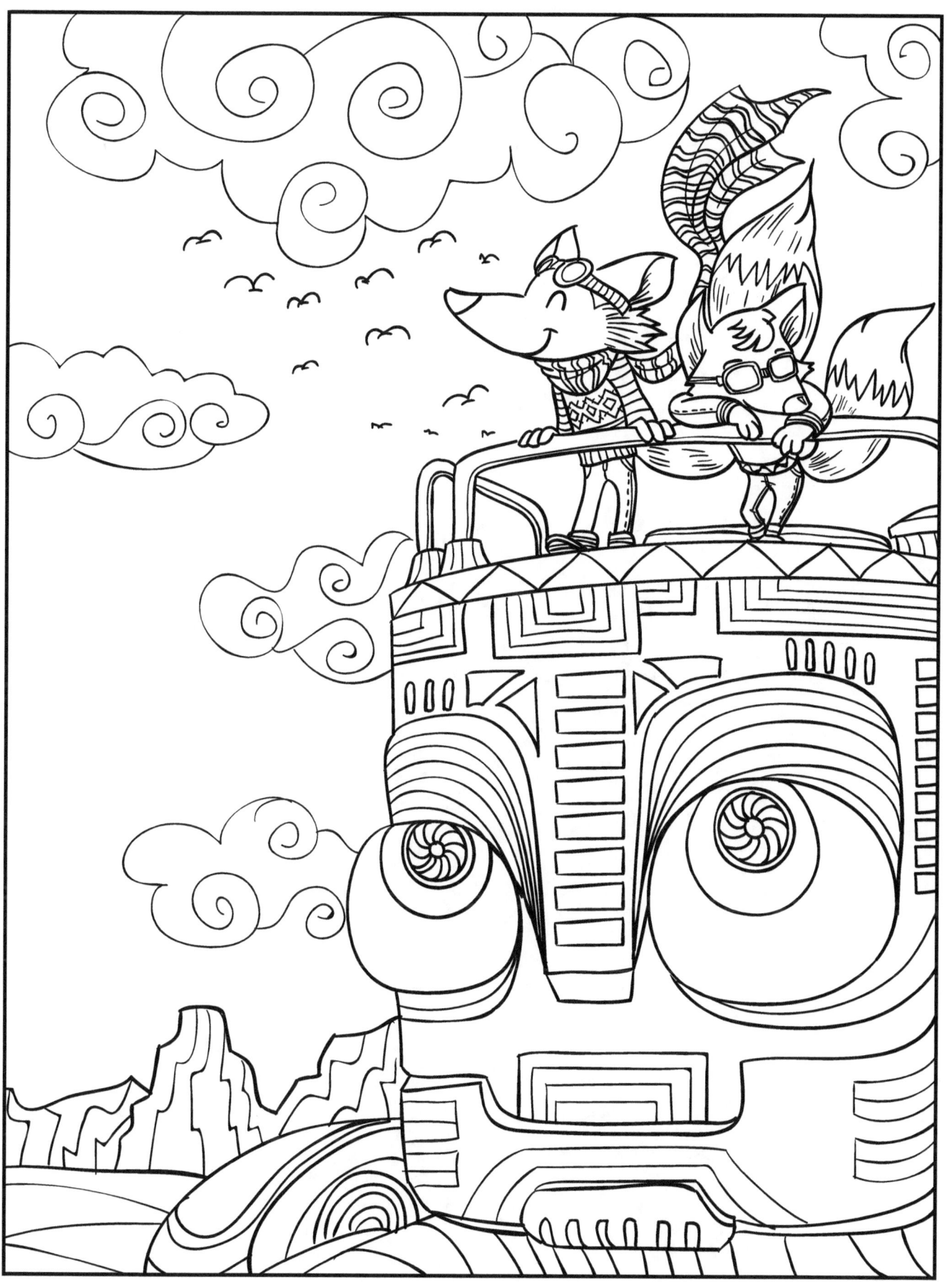

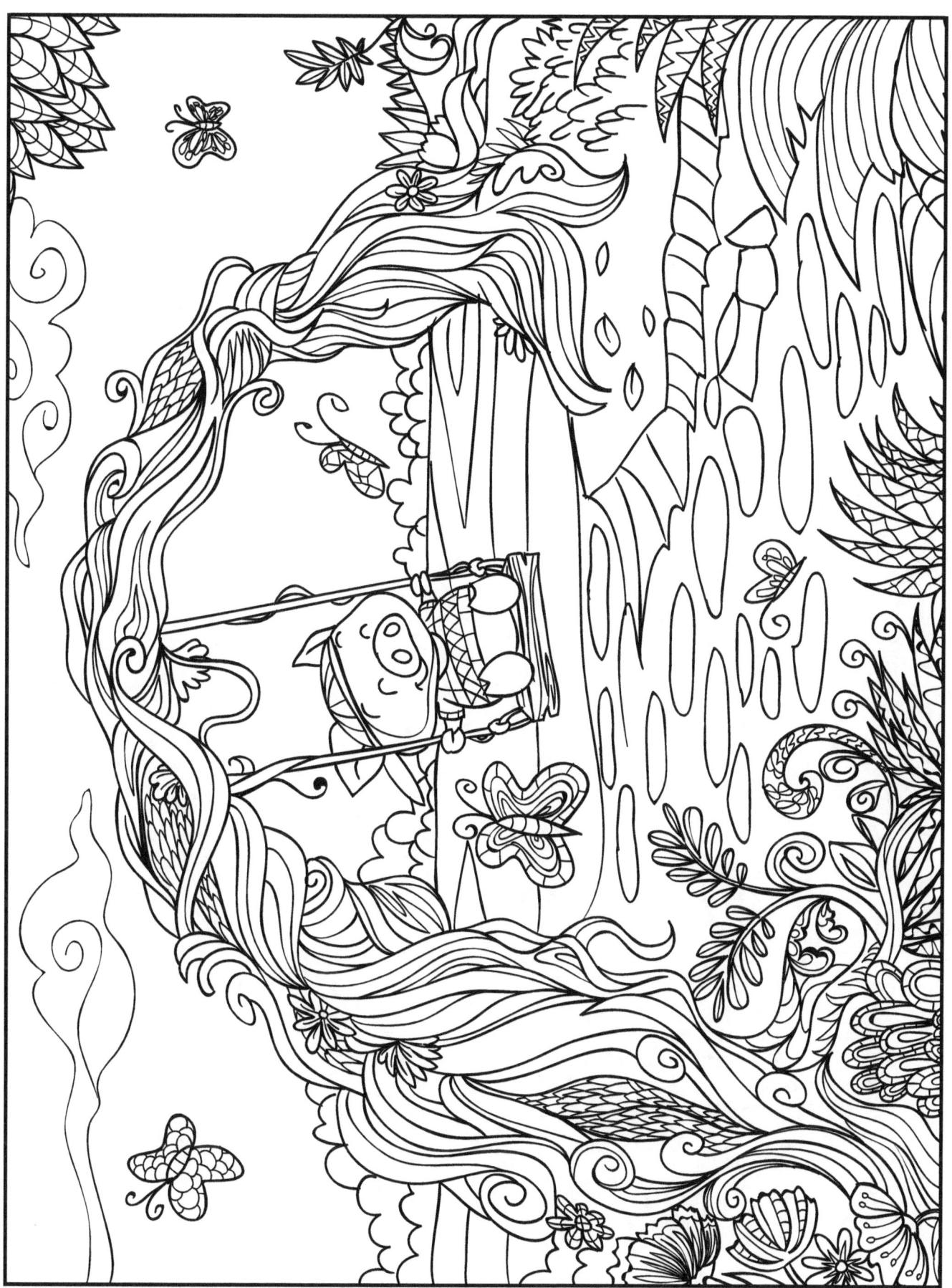

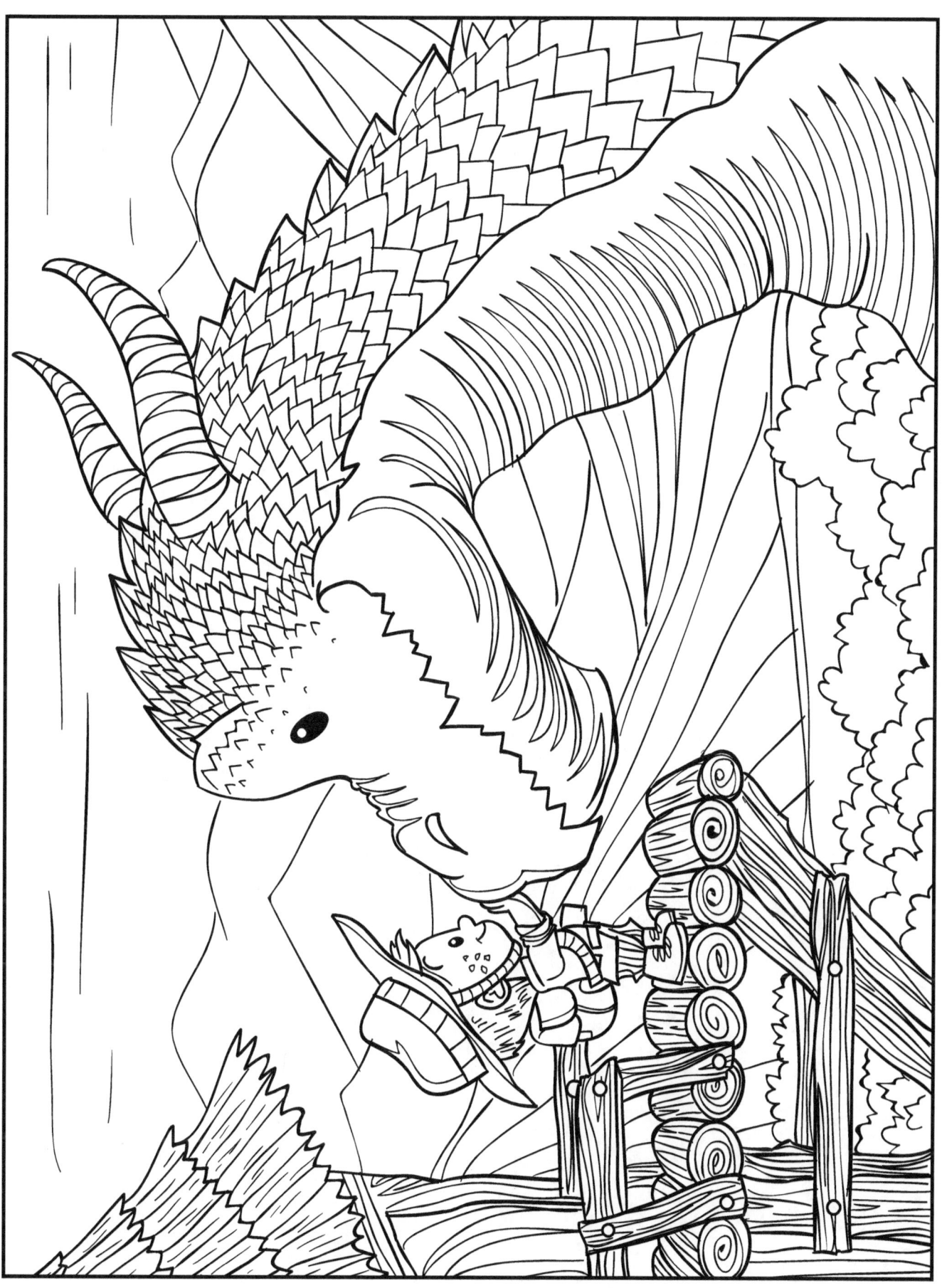

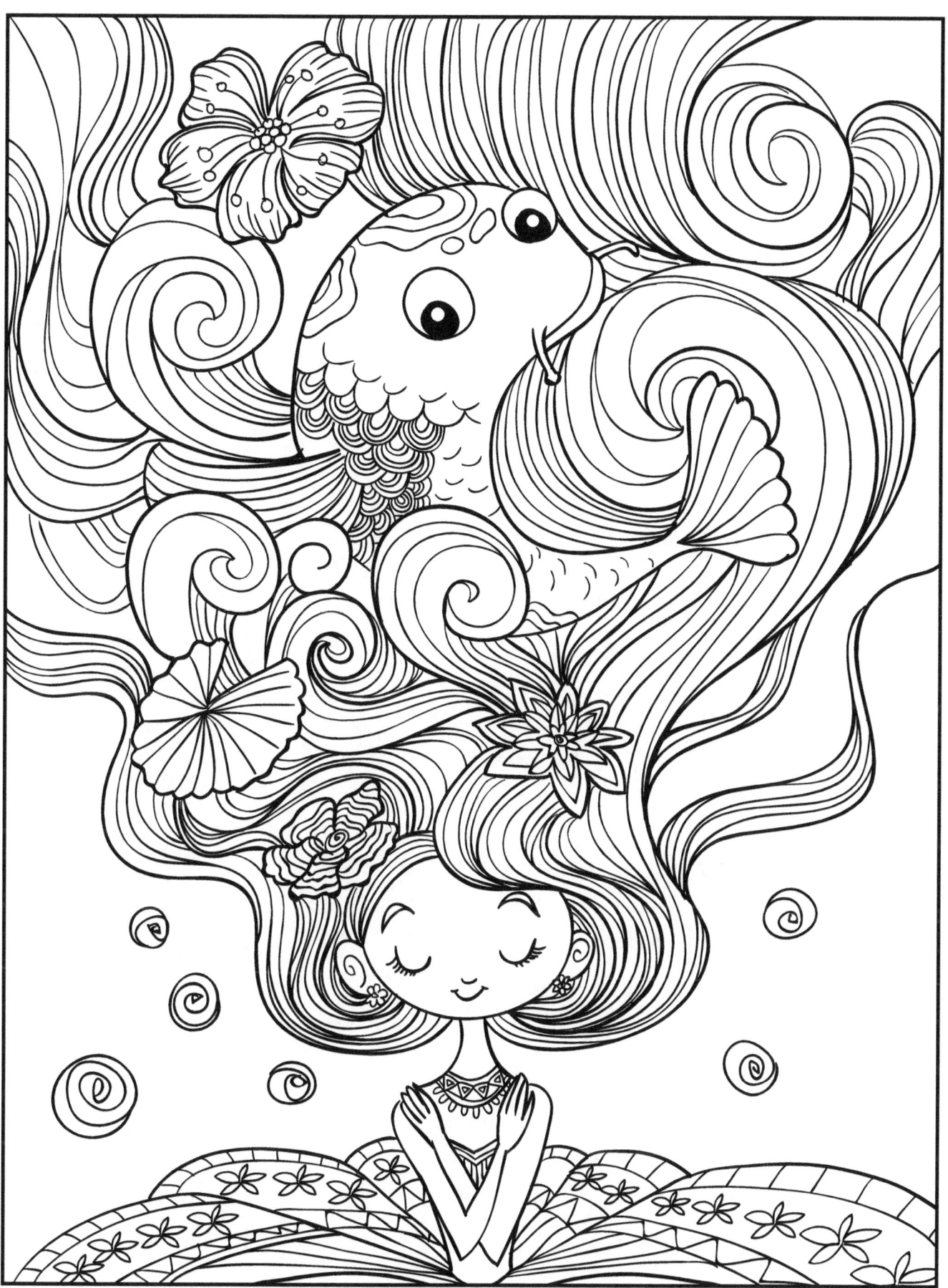

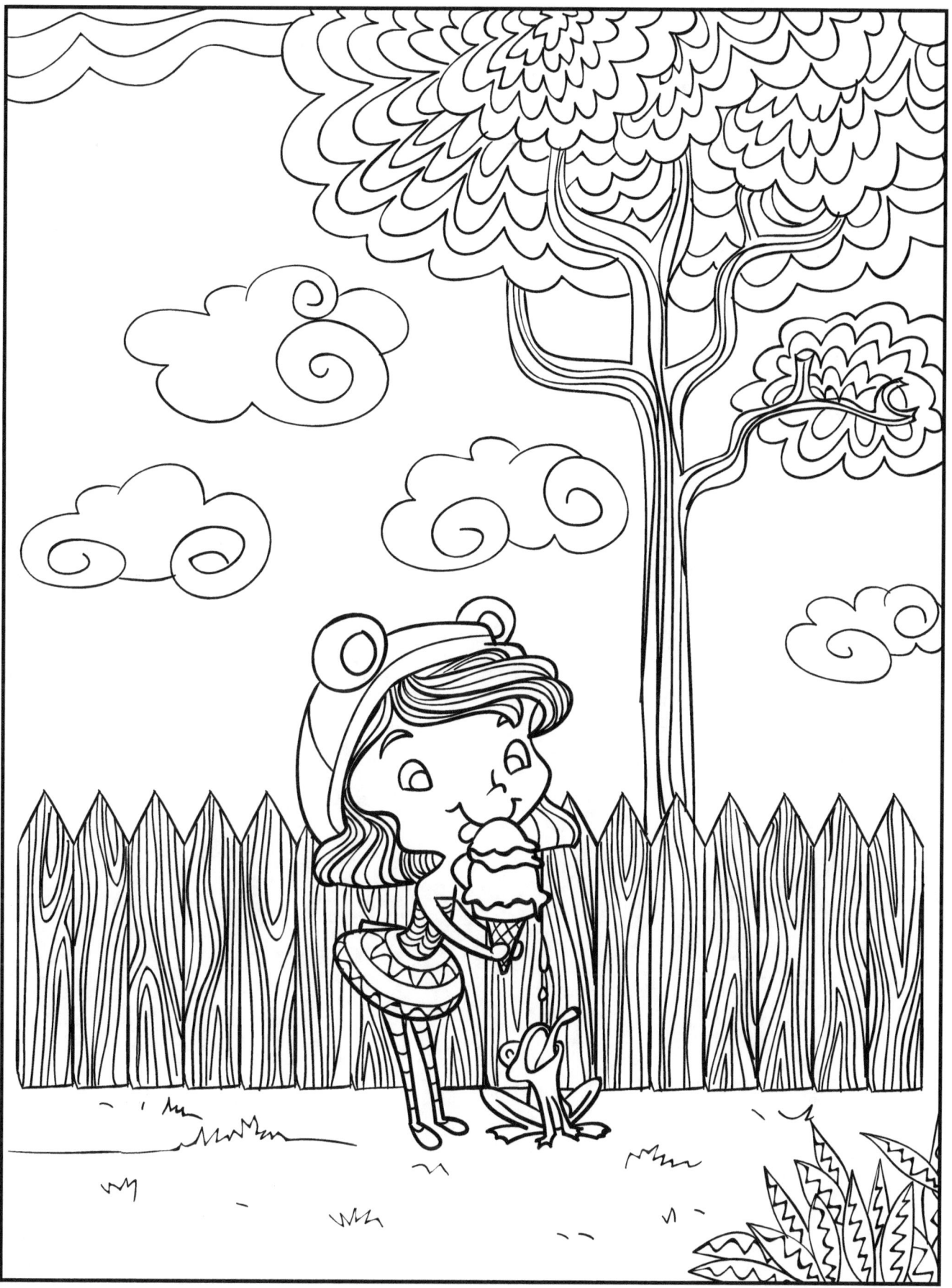

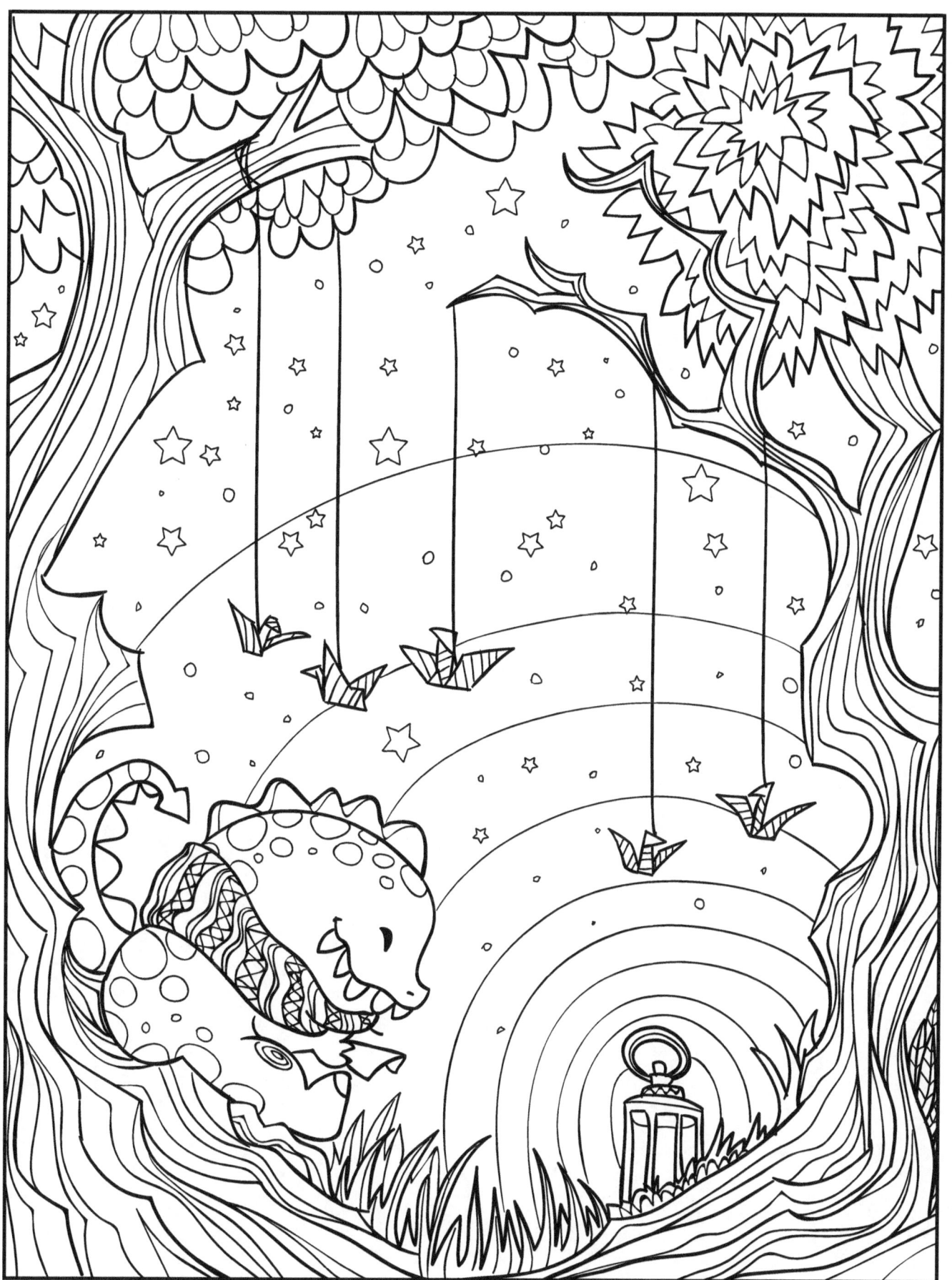

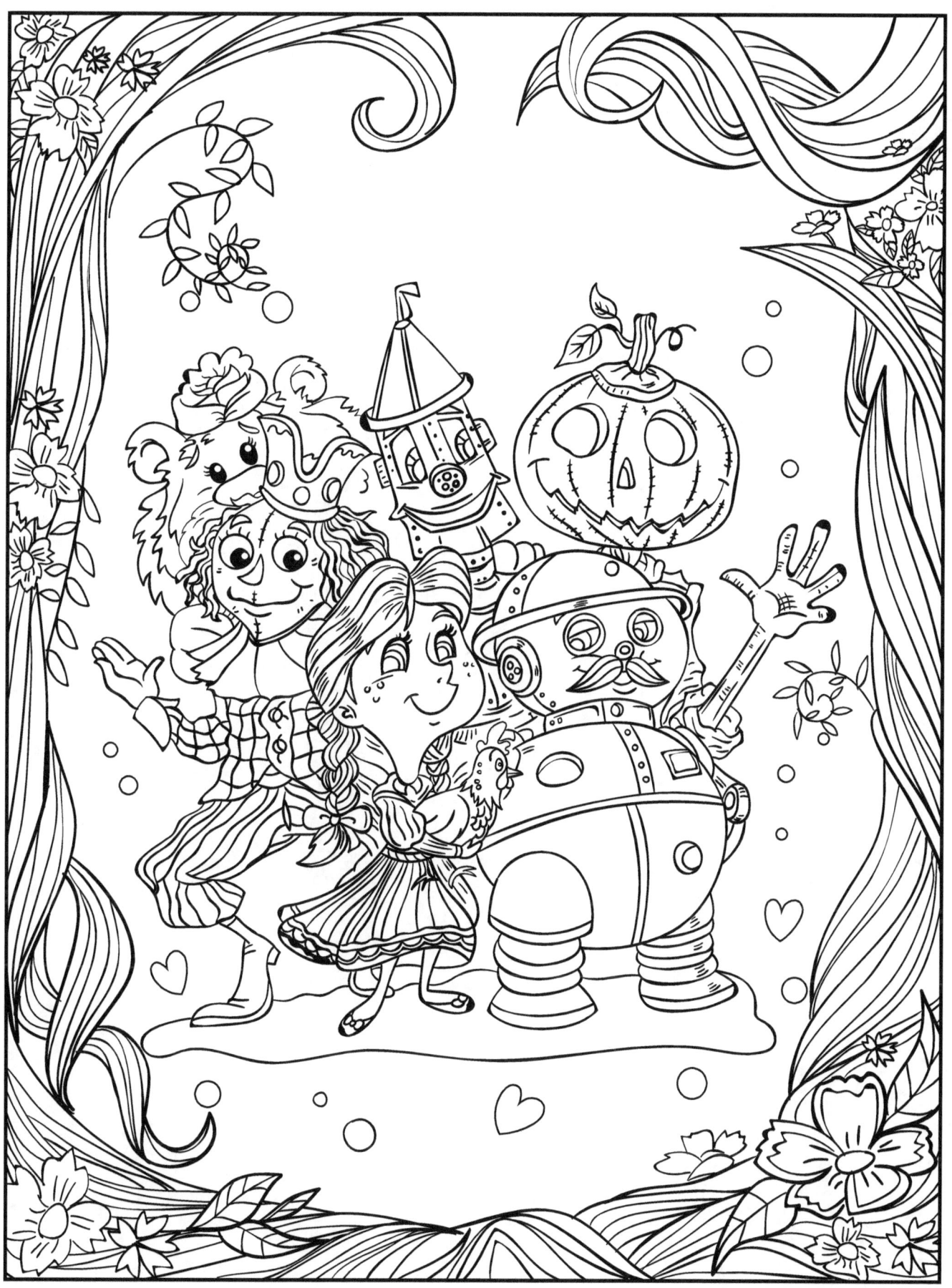

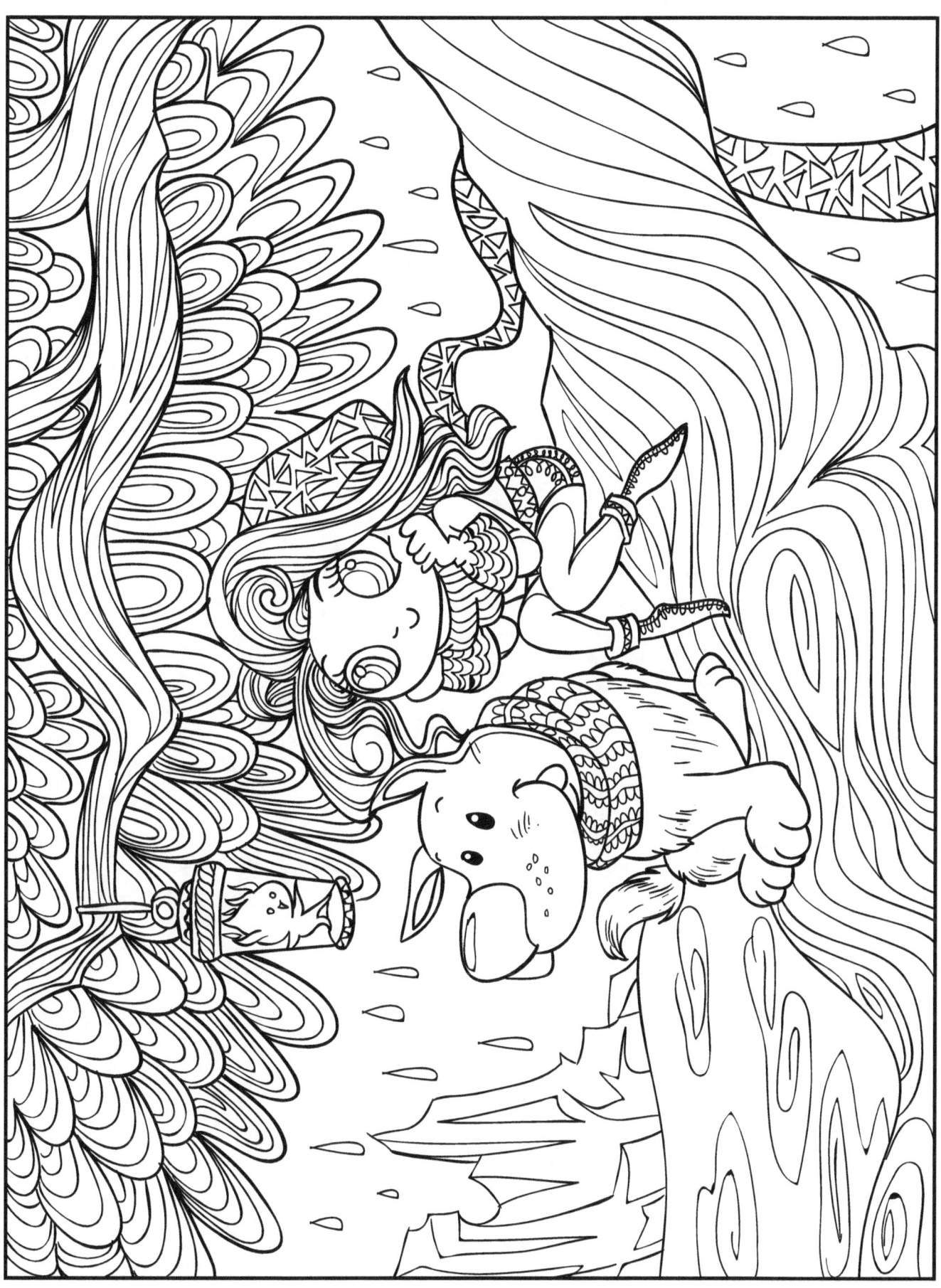

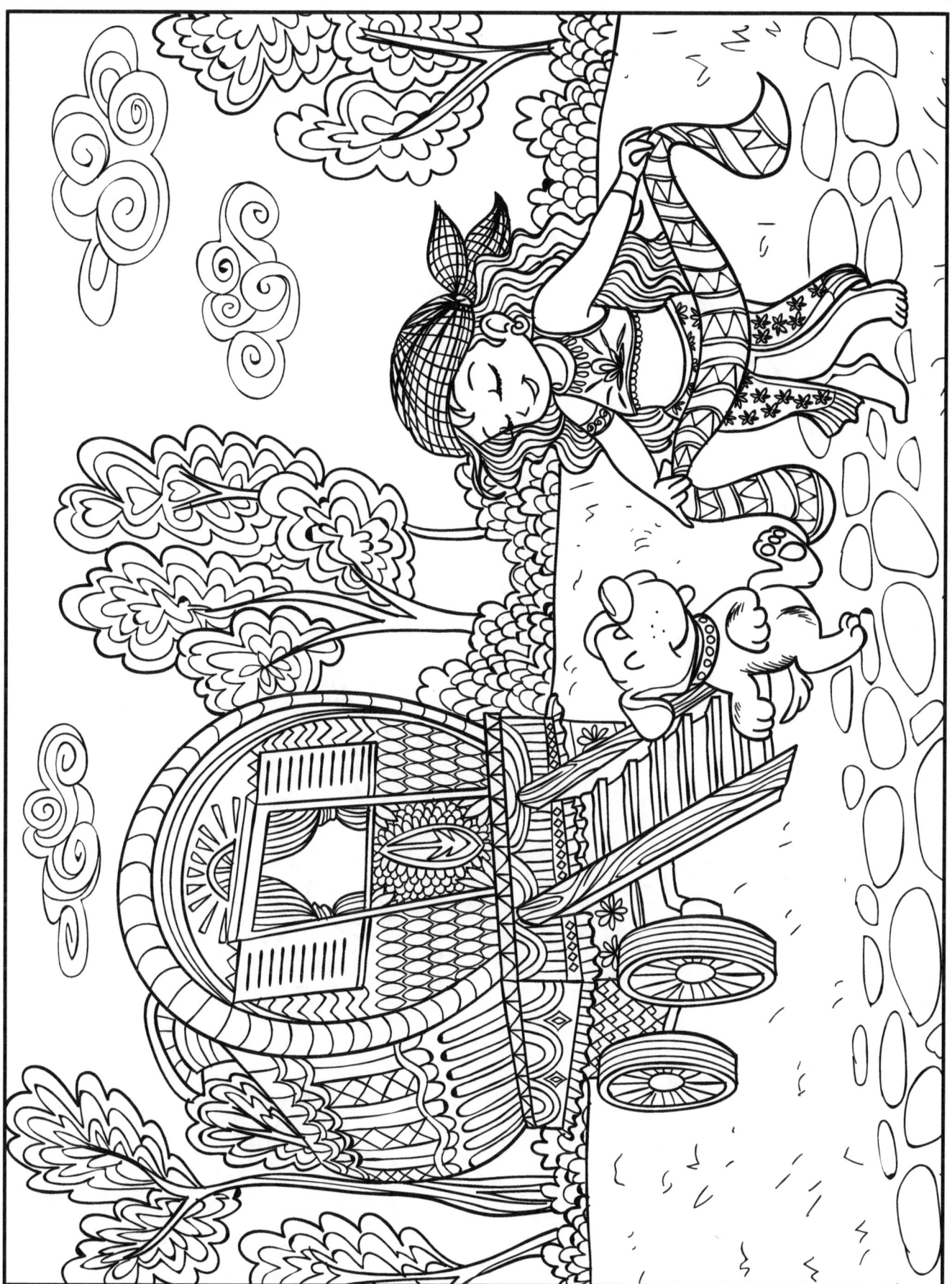

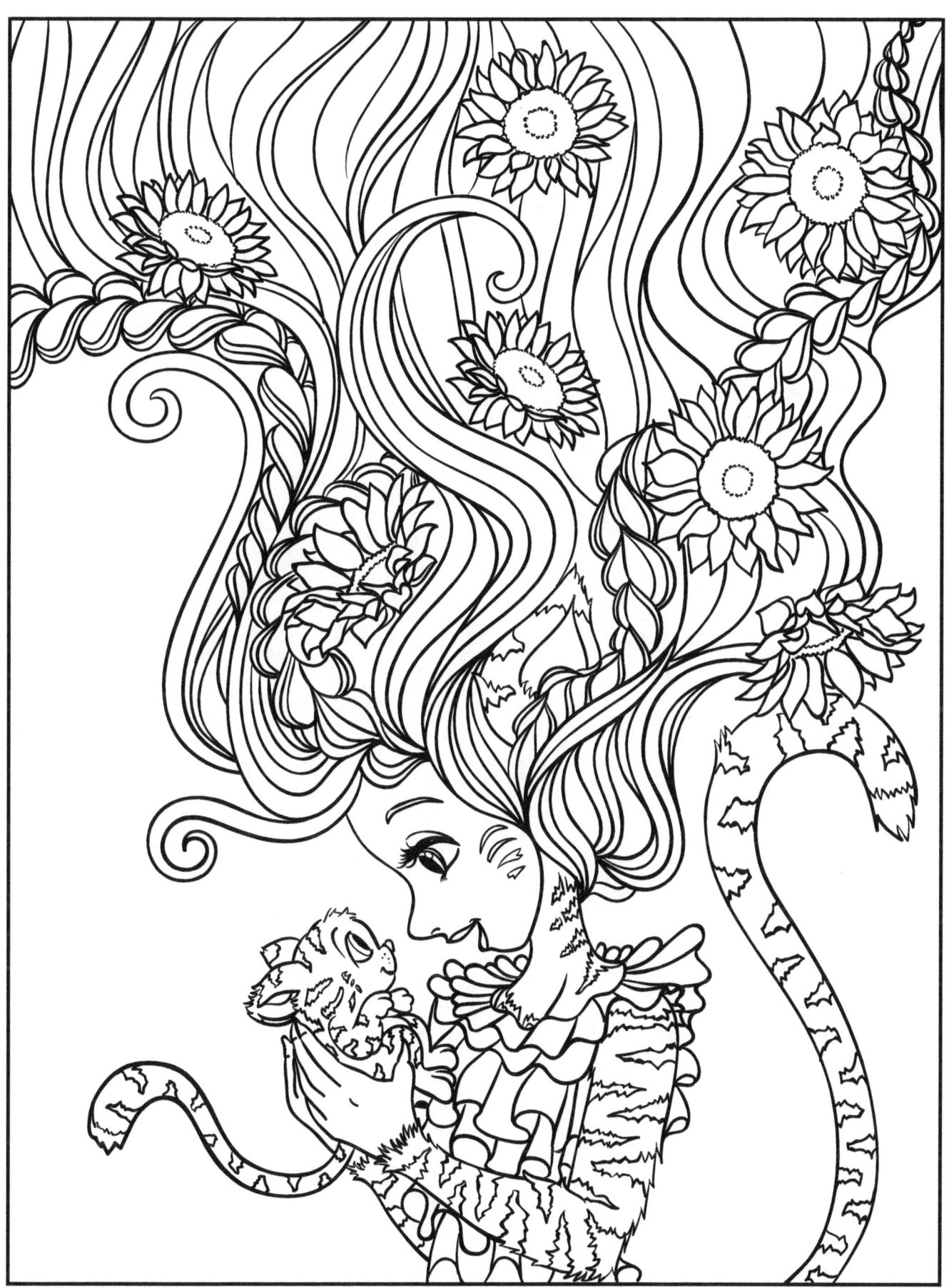

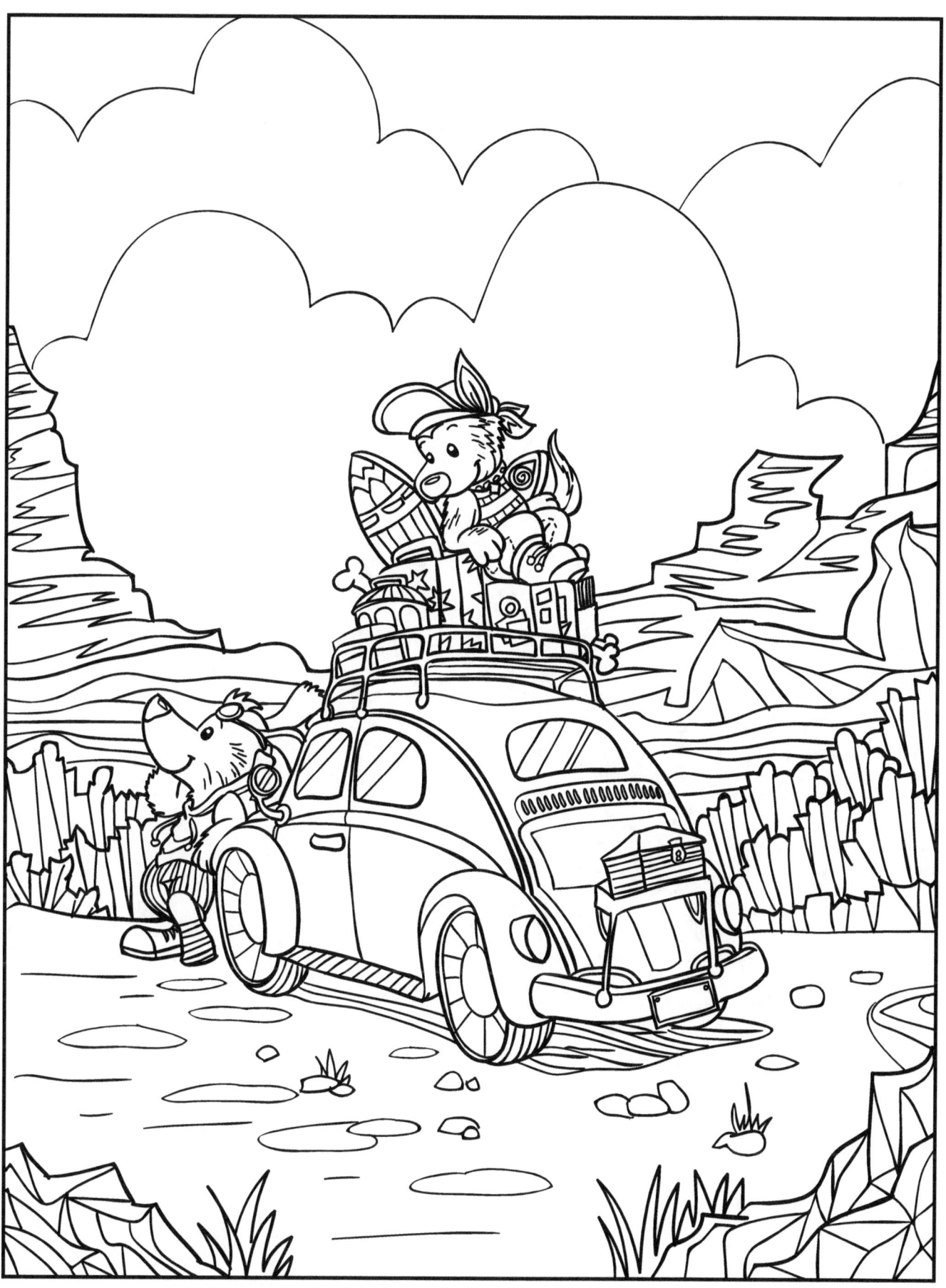

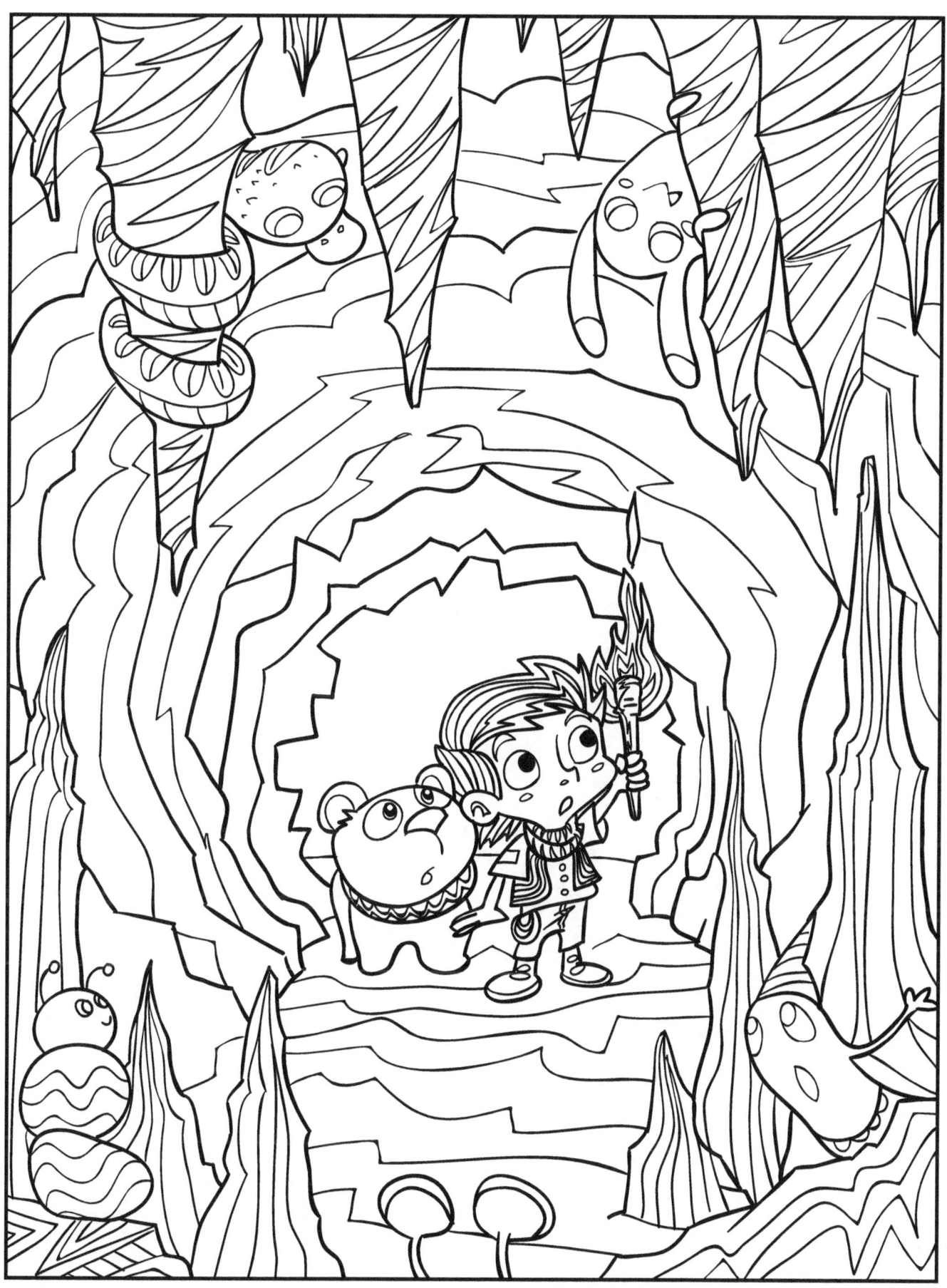

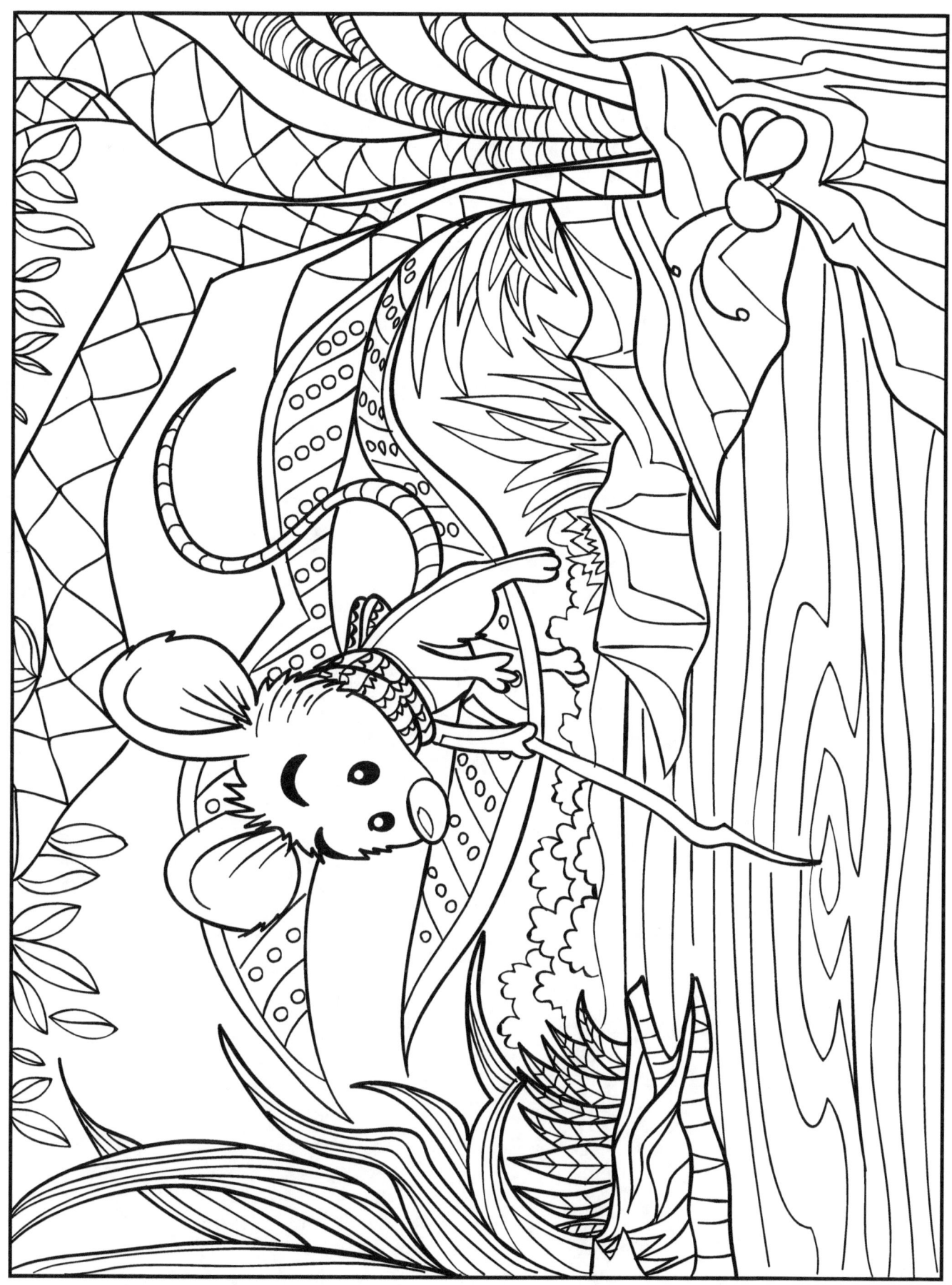

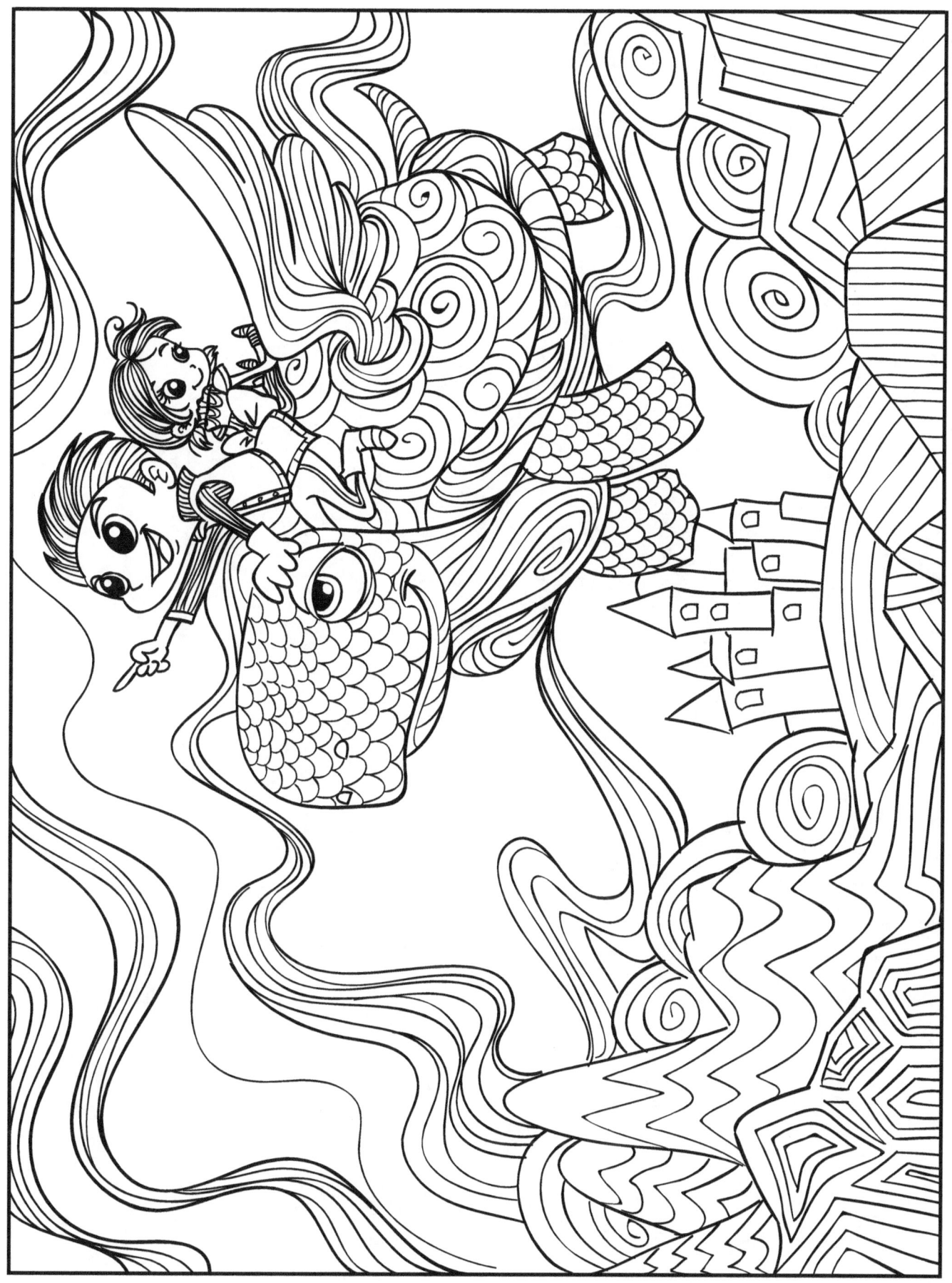

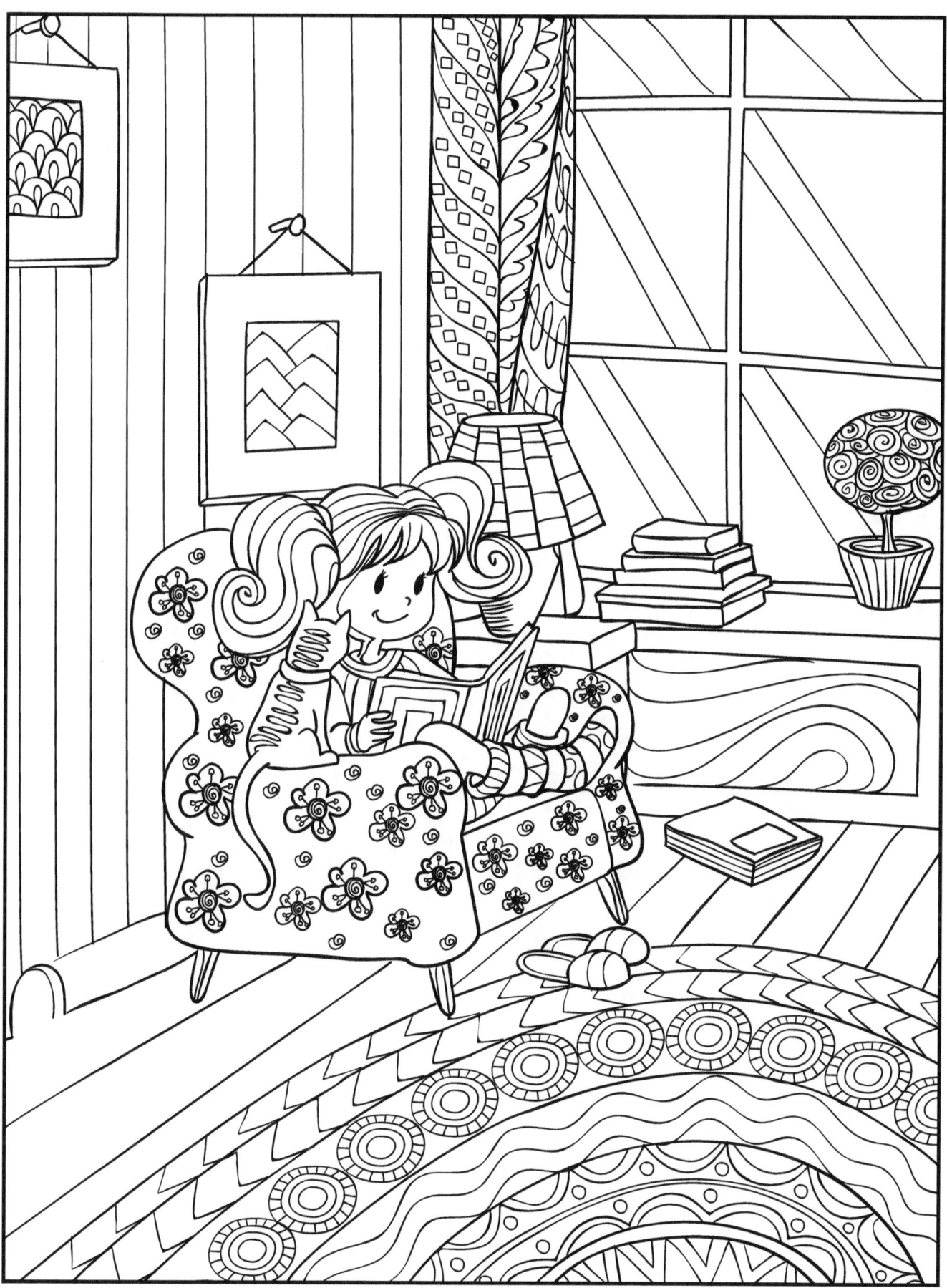

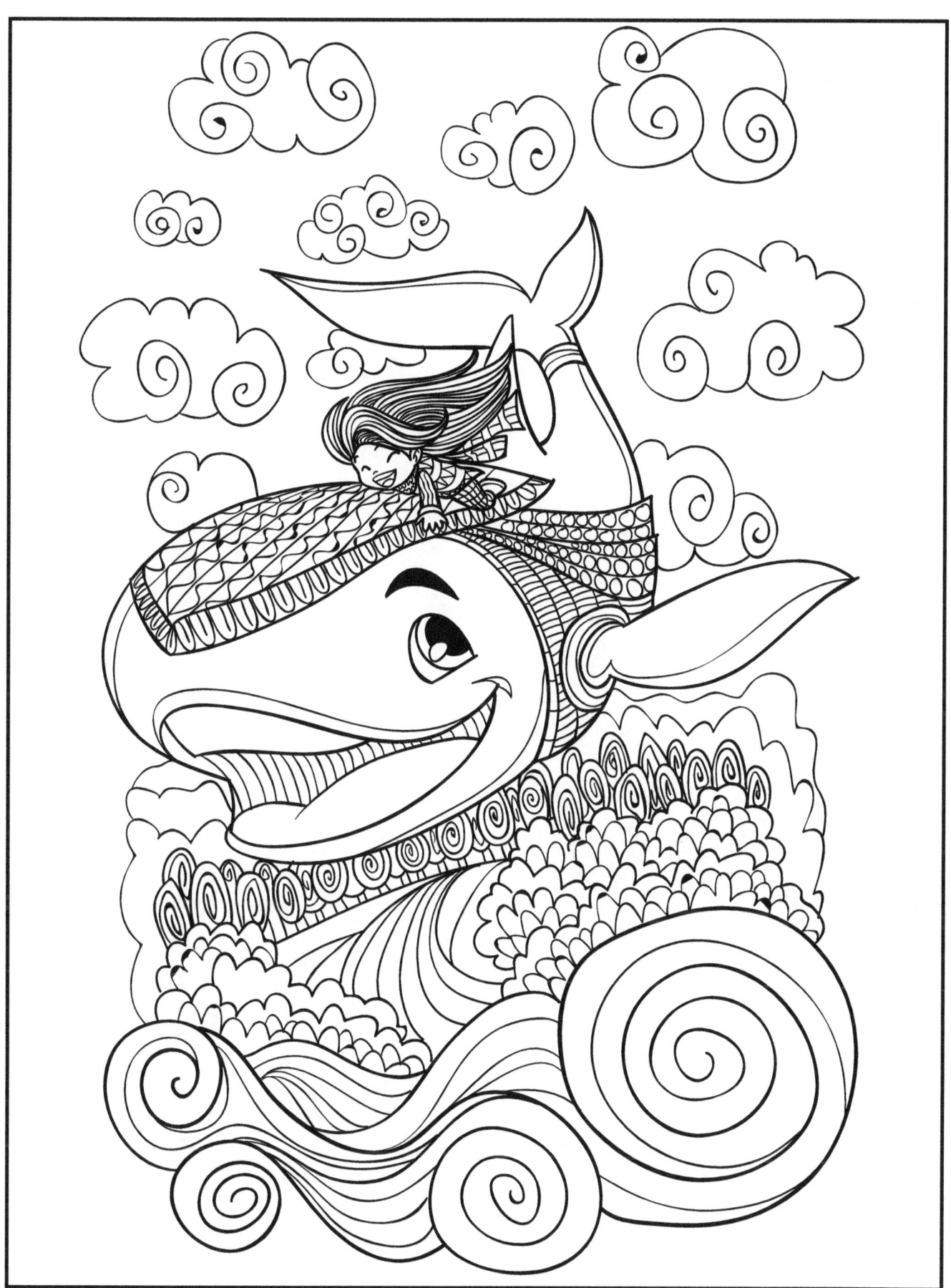

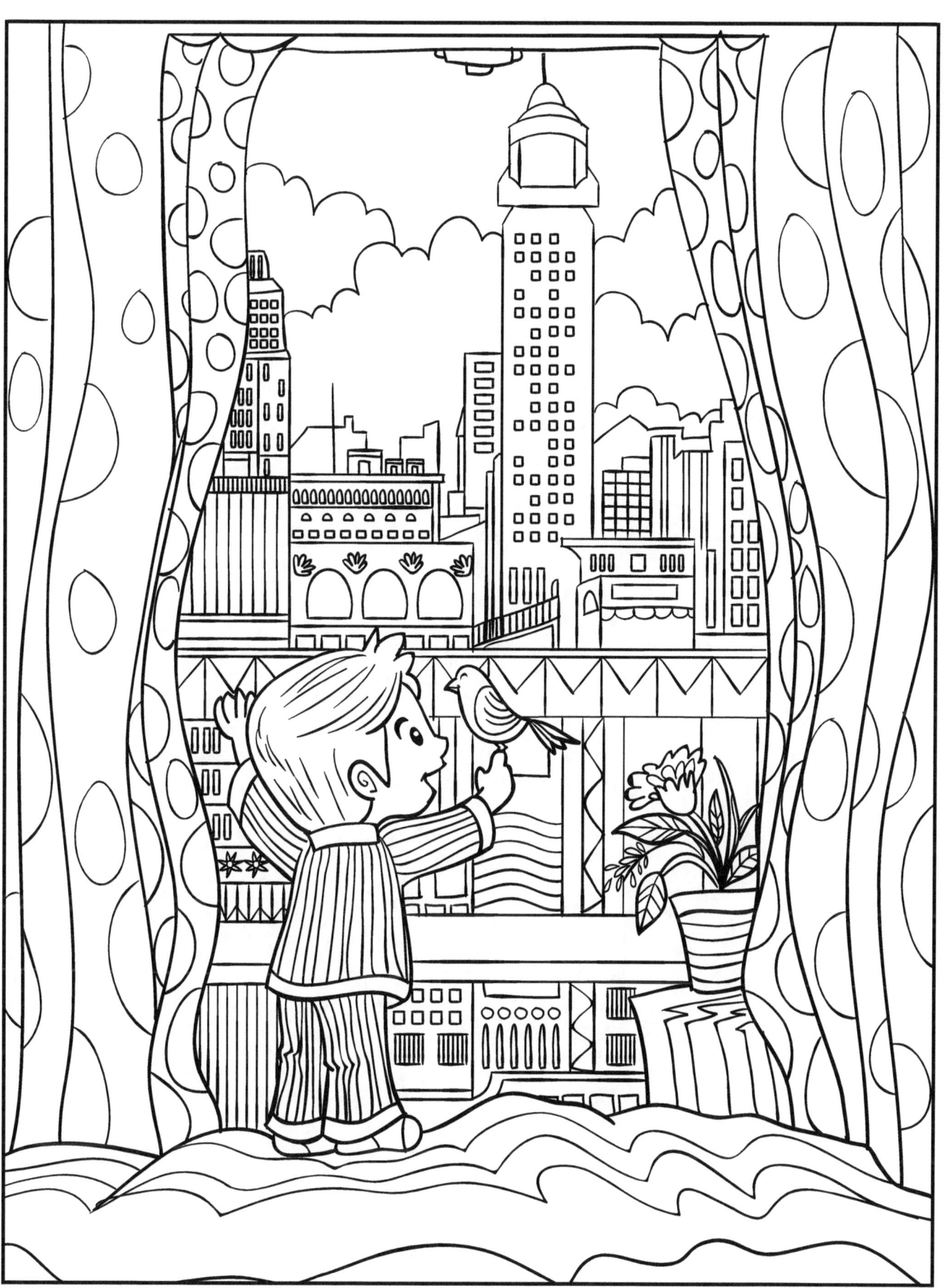

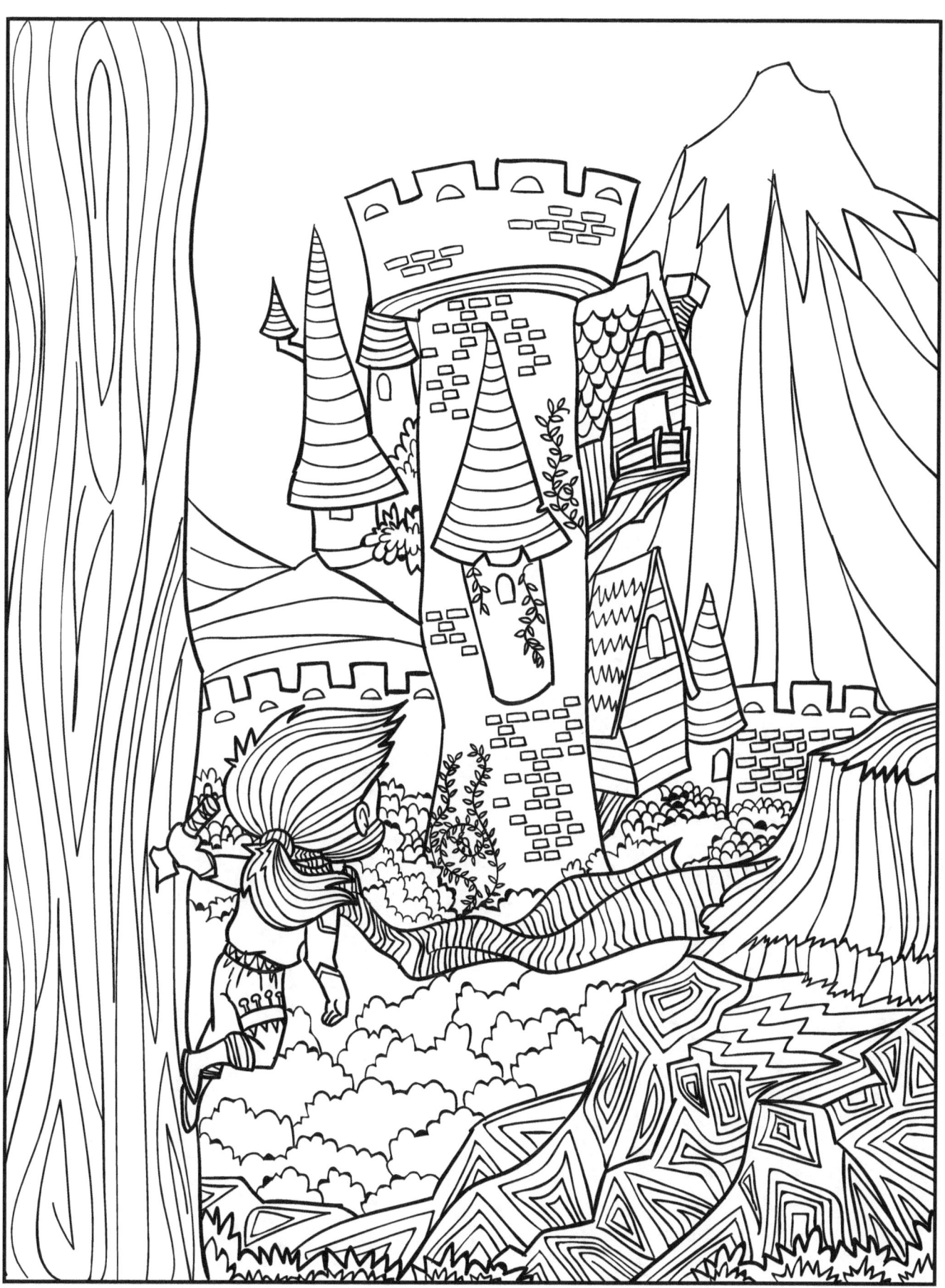

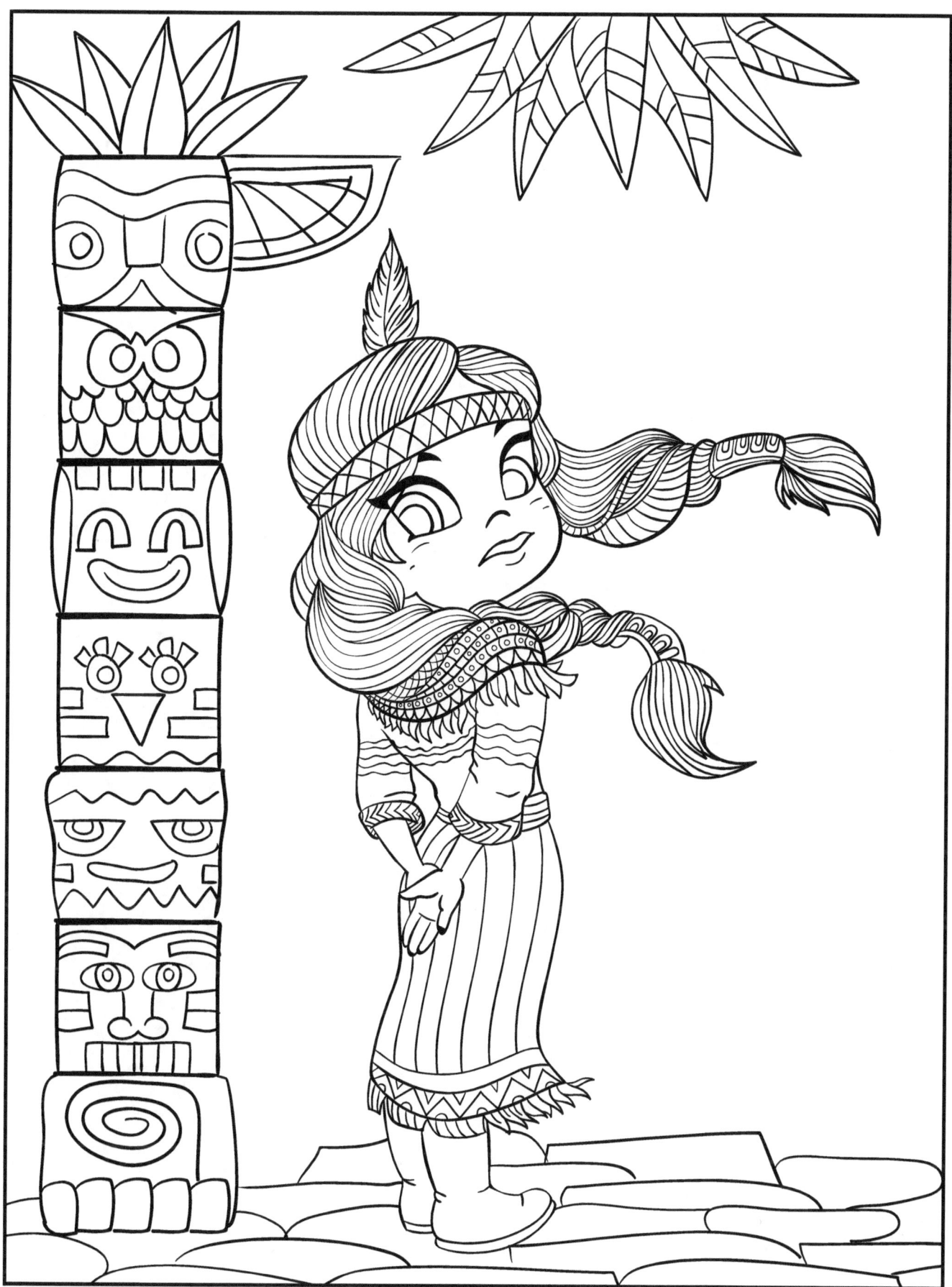

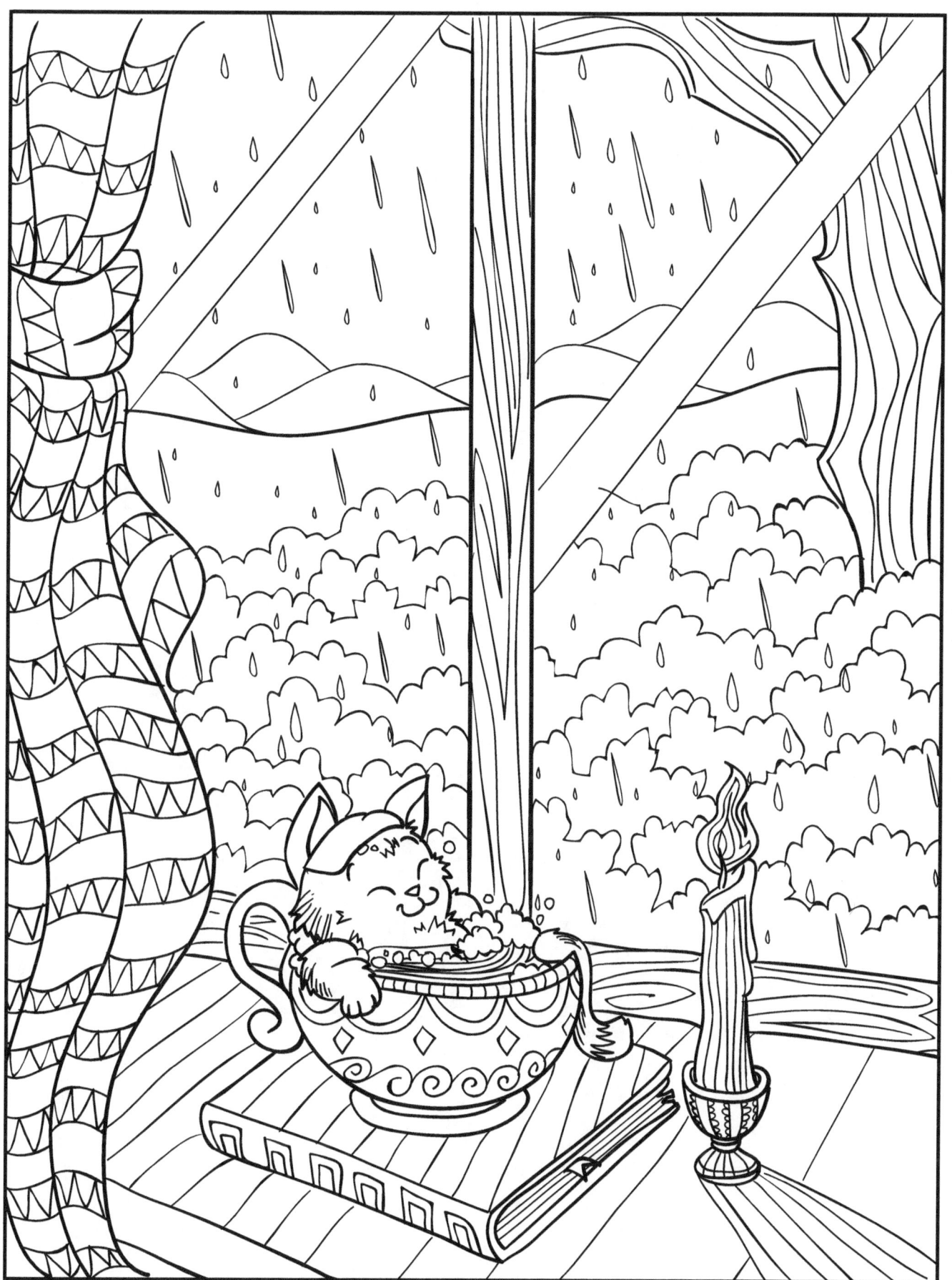

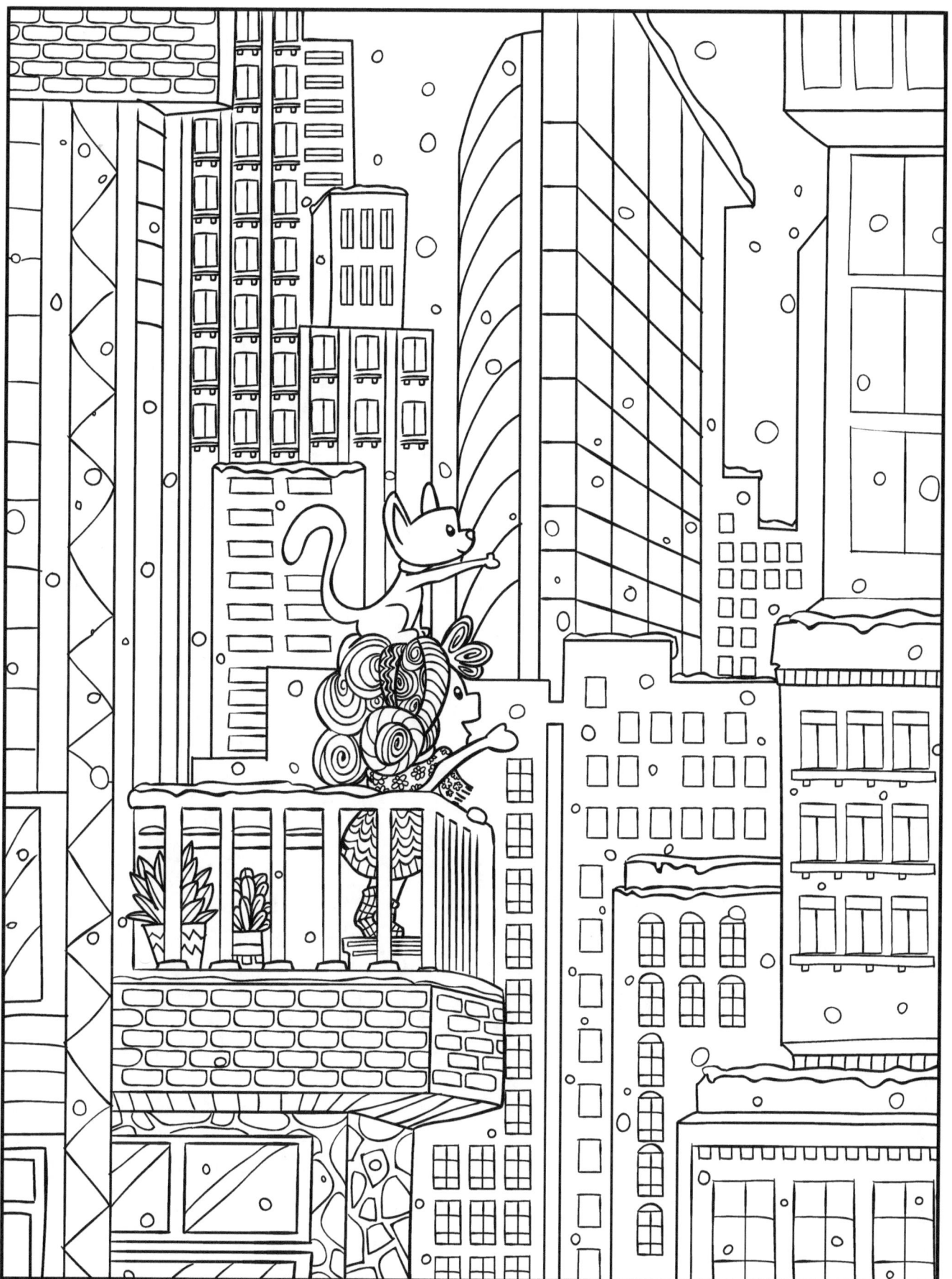

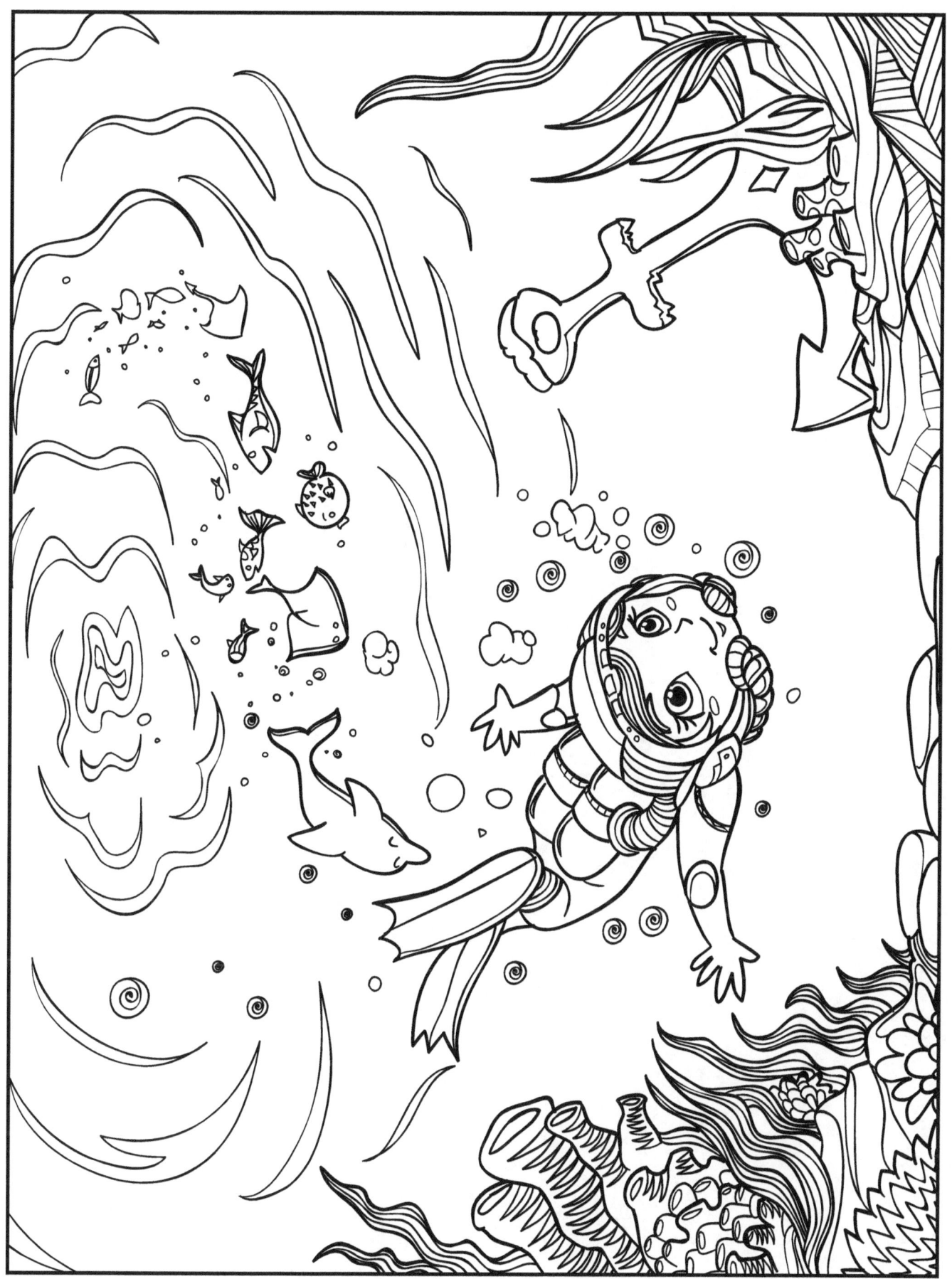

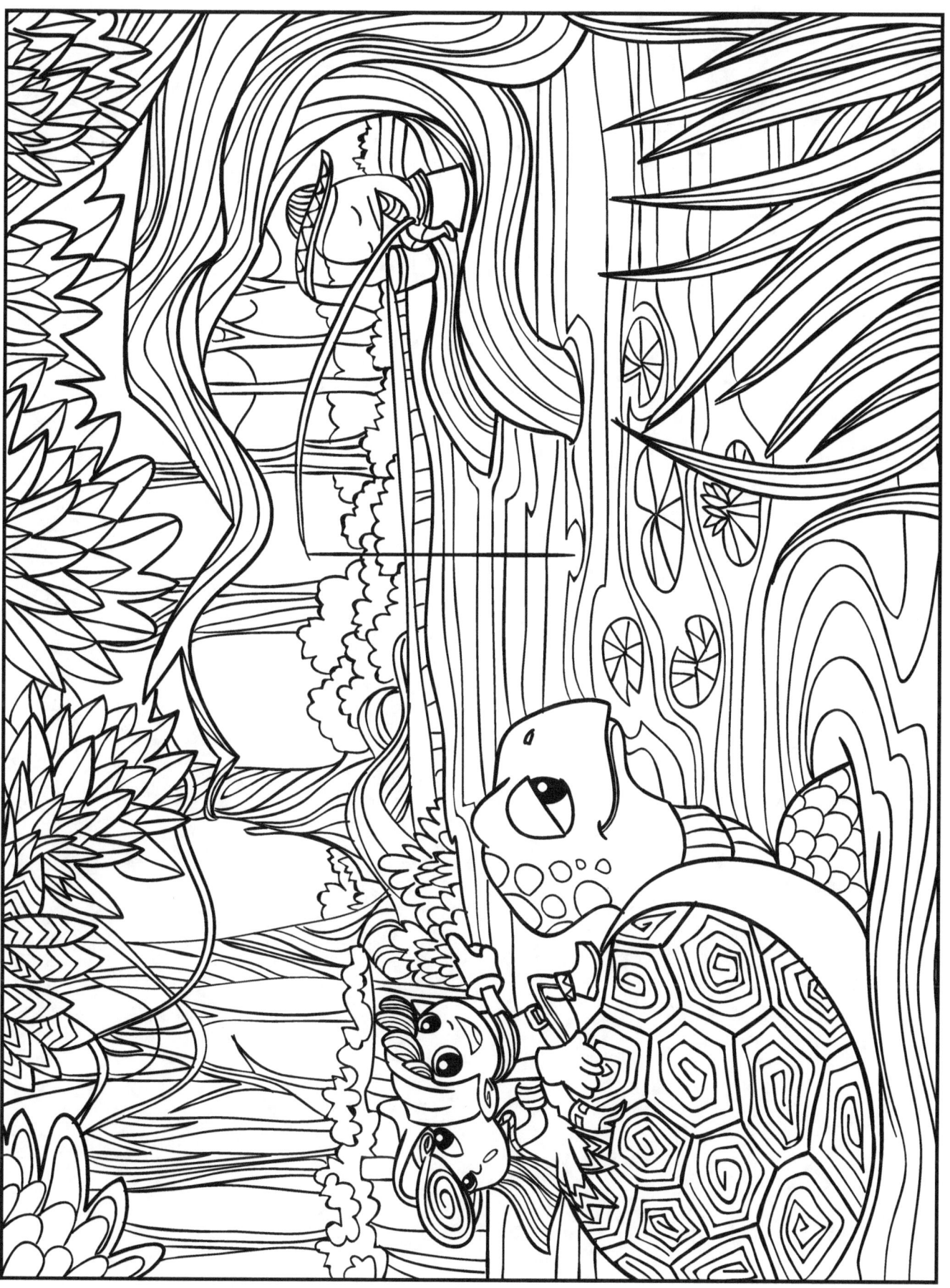

Hope you enjoyed this book!

Please join our coloring group to stay updated with our work in progress, as well as get notified when we have special book promotion available!

Free coloring pages are also available for you to download once you join the group.

Please sign up via the link below, or scan the barcode from your mobile phone.

http://coloring.davlinpublishing.com